T0194096

From the Pastor's Pen

A 120-Day Devotional Journey

SAMUEL G. MAY

WESTBOW
PRESS®
A DIVISION OF THOMAS NELSON
& ZONDERVAN

WestBow Press books may be ordered through booksellers or by contacting:

WestBow Press
A Division of Thomas Nelson & Zondervan
1663 Liberty Drive
Bloomington, IN 47403
www.westbowpress.com
1 (866) 928-1240

ISBN: 978-1-9736-1802-7 (sc)
ISBN: 978-1-9736-1801-0 (hc)
ISBN: 978-1-9736-1803-4 (e)

Library of Congress Control Number: 2018901470

Print information available on the last page.

WestBow Press rev. date: 02/16/2018

Preface

The road of life is rather winding, and it has its ups and downs, even for a beloved child of God. This book is more than just a devotional. It is a companion to travel with you on that road. It's a reminder of things you probably already know but need to hear again in the moment. One feature of the book is the seemingly random *order* of the topics covered, but again, that's life! You never know what lies ahead when the sun comes up—another adventure with the Lord, another page in your book!

To get the most out of your 120-day journey, there are a few things that you should note. First, the pages are not dated but they are numbered so that you can make a note in the table of contents of any days that especially spoke to you and you want to find them easily to go back to them again or maybe share them with someone.

You can begin at any time, and if you miss some days, you can pick right back up where you left off. Each day begins with the devotional, and then you will find a section for journaling for that day. At the top of this section, you will find the title "A Journal of My Journey for (Date)

." This is where you will enter the date for that day's journal entry. It's a way to help keep track of your history with God!

Most of the scripture references are from the King James Version of the Bible. You may prefer a different translation for your daily devotions or enjoy comparing translations. Therefore, as an enhancement to your devotional time, you may also want to read the verses for the day from your favorite translation or maybe even several different translations.

It will also help if you can find a quiet time and place to go through the book. A few days will have a prayer included, but every day is a good day to pray! Begin with prayer and end with prayer. Talk to the Lord and allow time for Him to talk to you through His Word!

Even when you have "finished" this part of your journey, you will have it to refer back to from now on. The truths of the Word of God never go out of date!

Finally, as with everything good the Lord does for us, it is not only for us to enjoy and benefit from but also for us to share with others. Be blessed and be a blessing. Allow the Lord to minister through you to others with these pages.

My prayer for you is that each day will bring the fresh fire of His Word upon your soul and that you will go through that day rejoicing over the truth He revealed to you, eager to share it with some fellow traveler along life's highway. As you walk with the Lord, you will take life as He intended—one day at a time!

Contents

1. Enjoy the Journey!

As we journey forth into the great unknown, the thing that keeps us in perfect peace is our knowledge of the great known—our God!

We were created in God's image, made only a little lower than the angels! God's intention for you is to have dominion over this world.

First Chronicles 16:7–12 (KJV) says, "Then on that day David delivered first this psalm to thank the LORD into the hand of Asaph and his brethren. Give thanks unto the LORD, call upon his name, make known his deeds among the people. Sing unto him, sing Psalm unto him, talk ye of all his wondrous works. Glory ye in his holy name: let the heart of them rejoice that seek the LORD. Seek the LORD and his strength, seek his face continually. Remember his marvelous works that he hath done, his wonders, and the judgments of his mouth."

When you read those verses, a couple of things really stand out—His wondrous works and His marvelous works. When you take time to see God in every day, you will see the wonder as well as the marvels of His love and care for you!

Does that mean a trouble-free life? Not in this world! King David knew his share of trouble, but this psalm is a reminder to you to enjoy the journey and to find our Maker's wondrous and marvelous works each step of the way. Enjoy the journey!

A Journal of My Journey for (Date)

_____

_____

_____

_____

_____

_____

_____

_____

_____

_____

_____

_____

_____

_____

2. Today Is a Good Day

Today may have its challenges, but there is some good in it because God is in it! Not only that, but God made today and every day, so there has to be something good in today since every good thing comes from God! That is why you can always say, "Today is a good day!"

Psalm 34:8 (KJV) says, "O taste and see that the LORD is good: blessed is the man that trusteth in him."

The sweetest of all God's blessings is salvation. Once we become Christians, every day is full of God's goodness. You have the reason of reasons to rejoice and be glad every day!

Psalm 118:21–29 (KJV) says,
I will praise thee: for thou hast heard me, and art become my salvation. The stone which the builders refused is become the head stone of the corner. This is the LORD'S doing; it is marvellous in our eyes. This is the day which the LORD hath made; we will rejoice and be glad in it. Save now, I beseech thee, O LORD: O LORD, I beseech thee, send now prosperity. Blessed be he that cometh in the name of the LORD: we have blessed you out of the house of the LORD. God is the LORD, which hath showed us light: bind the sacrifice with cords, even unto the horns of the altar. Thou art my God, and I will praise thee: thou art my God, I will exalt thee. O give thanks unto the LORD; for he is good: for his mercy endureth for ever.

Oh give thanks to the Lord, for He is good, and always remember to say, "Today is a good day."

A Journal of My Journey for (Date)

_____

_____

_____

_____

_____

_____

_____

_____

_____

_____

_____

_____

_____

_____

_____

3. The Great Adventure

Adventure: an unusual and exciting, typically hazardous, experience or activity.

That sounds about like life, doesn't it? Let's break it down. Unusual? That is for sure. You never know what a usual day looks like because as soon as you define normal, it gets redefined. Life doesn't stay the same as much as we would sometimes like for it to.

What else can we say about life? Exciting? Yes, life is certainly filled with excitement. This is easy for small children to see. They can become excited over the simplest things, and an adventure is waiting around every corner for them. But then as you grow older, you can easily lose that sense of adventure and miss out on so much that each day holds.

And finally, that third part is typically hazardous. Yep, the enemy of your soul is always looking for an opening, a way to intersect with your life and do what he does. But never let the devil keep you from living the life that God has given you.

Proverbs 25:2 (KJV) says, "It is the glory of God to conceal a thing: but the honour of kings is to search out a matter."

You are a king and priest to the Lord God Almighty, and He has you on a quest, an adventure, almost like a treasure hunt. But the treasure is well worth the adventure! You do not know what a day will bring forth, but you do know who brings forth each day.

Glory only in the Lord. That is the only sure thing! Everything else is just part of the adventure.

A Journal of My Journey for (Date)

_____

_____

_____

_____

_____

_____

_____

_____

_____

_____

_____

_____

_____

_____

_____

4. You're Not Alone

Sometimes you may feel you are all alone in this world, even in a crowd! This can be the result of different things, but it could be that you have been hurt or let down in the past. Maybe without even realizing it, you have put a barrier around your heart to keep any more of that hurt from getting in. The problem is that the same barrier that keeps the hurt out also keeps the help out!

Even from the beginning of time, God said, "It's not good that man should be alone." Just as Adam needed a helpmate and God created the institution of marriage and thus the family, He also created the church and made Jesus the head of the church. We need one another, and even though it is risky (and you will probably get hurt somewhere along the way), it is essential.

Ecclesiastes 4:9–12 (KJV) says, "Two *are* better than one; because they have a good reward for their labour. For if they fall, the one will lift up his fellow: but woe to him *that is* alone when he falleth; for *he hath* not another to help him up. Again, if two lie together, then they have heat: but how can one be warm *alone*? And if one prevail against him, two shall withstand him; and a threefold cord is not quickly broken" (emphasis added).

The next time you feel all alone, ask the Lord to show you the ones He has put in your life. Open up your heart and allow some heavenly help to come in by way of His helpers. The help you need may be right outside of your heart just waiting for an opening, and once you realize this truth, you may also realize that you're not alone!

A Journal of My Journey for (Date)

_____

5. Lord, Don't You Even Care?

There is another aspect to feeling alone in this world that goes beyond shutting out others, living in this world without experiencing the reality of your Creator's love and care for you each day. That can actually creep in upon you more easily than you might think. We see plenty of examples of it in God's Word as we shall see, but you have probably had some of those moments yourself!

When God was delivering His people, Israel, from Egypt, they came up to the edge of the Red Sea with Pharaoh's army in hot pursuit.

Exodus 14:12 (KJV) says, "*Is* not this the word that we did tell thee in Egypt, saying, Let us alone, that we may serve the Egyptians? For *it had been* better for us to serve the Egyptians, than that we should die in the wilderness" (emphasis added).

God supernaturally delivers His people. After three days they are complaining about the water, and after a month and a half, it has gotten to this point.

Exodus 16:2–3 (KJV) says, "And the whole congregation of the children of Israel murmured against Moses and Aaron in the wilderness: And the children of Israel said unto them, Would to God we had died by the hand of the LORD in the land of Egypt, when we sat by the flesh pots, *and* when we did eat bread to the full; for ye have brought us forth into this wilderness, to kill this whole assembly with hunger" (emphasis added).

Jesus' disciples were not immune to those moments of thinking that the Lord did not even care about them.

Mark 4:37 (KJV) says,
And there arose a great storm of wind, and the waves beat into the ship, so that it was now full. And he was in the hinder part of the ship, asleep on a pillow: and they awake him, and say unto him, Master, carest thou not that we perish? And he arose, and rebuked the wind, and said unto the sea, Peace, be still. And the wind ceased, and there was a great calm. And he said unto them, Why are ye so fearful? how is it that ye have no faith?

God makes a way! He will show Himself as strong on your behalf. He will never leave you or forsake you. He loves you with an everlasting love, and you can cast all your care on Him, for He always cares for you!

A Journal of My Journey for (Date)

_____

_____

_____

_____

_____

_____

_____

_____

_____

_____

_____

_____

_____

_____

6. Songs from Heaven

Even though we cannot usually see into the spiritual realm or hardly ever hear what is going on there, we see the effects of the kingdom of God on the earth in and around God's children!

Jesus taught Nicodemus (and us) this lesson when He was teaching him about being born again.

John 3:8 (KJV) says, "The wind bloweth where it listeth, and thou hearest the sound thereof, but canst not tell whence it cometh, and whither it goeth: so is every one that is born of the Spirit."

There is another way that we know what is going on in God's kingdom. He has revealed quite a bit about it in His Word! For instance, God is always in your midst, and He is rejoicing over you.

That's how much He loves you and cares for you.

Zephaniah 3:17 (KJV) says, "The LORD thy God in the midst of thee *is* mighty; he will save, he will rejoice over thee with joy; he will rest in his love, he will joy over thee with singing" (emphasis added).

Even though you cannot see it with your natural eyes, God will always provide you a place of refuge in His presence, and it includes His special playlist—heavenly songs of deliverance!

The Lord is your hiding place, your secret place, your place of refuge, the place where His song is being sung—about you!

Even if you can't hear the words of that heavenly song, it's enough just to know it is being sung. Fear not, for you are surrounded—surrounded by God's love and His songs of deliverance.

A Journal of My Journey for (Date)

_____

_____

_____

_____

_____

_____

_____

_____

_____

_____

_____

_____

_____

_____

7. He Knows Your Name

One thing that helps you to remember how much you mean to the Lord is the fact that He knows your name! That's right. The God who created everything and even now upholds all things by the Word of His power—He knows your name. And when He calls to you, He isn't saying, "Hey, you!" or "What was your name again?" No, He calls you by your name.

Isaiah 43:1–2 (KJV) says, "But now thus saith the LORD that created thee, O Jacob, and he that formed thee, O Israel, Fear not: for I have redeemed thee, I have called *thee* by thy name; thou *art* mine. When thou passest through the waters, I *will be* with thee; and through the rivers, they shall not overflow thee: when thou walkest through the fire, thou shalt not be burned; neither shall the flame kindle upon thee" (emphasis added).

It is important to note that there will still be some trials along the way. You will pass through the waters and through the fire, but God will be with you and not allow you to be consumed by the hard times. You may think at times, *If God really loves me, He will keep me from this trial*, but instead of delivering you out of a situation, He may deliver you *through* it. Trust in the Lord and feed on His faithfulness.

John 20:15–16 (KJV) says, "Jesus saith unto her, Woman, why weepest thou? whom seekest thou? She, supposing him to be the gardener, saith unto him, Sir, if thou have borne him hence, tell me where thou hast laid him, and I will take him away. Jesus saith unto her, Mary. She turned herself, and saith unto him, Rabboni; which is to say, Master."

Mary recognized Jesus when He called her by her name. Jesus knows your name, and He is calling to you. Listen to the voice of your shepherd as He calls your name!

A Journal of My Journey for (Date)

_____

_____

_____

_____

_____

_____

_____

_____

_____

_____

_____

_____

_____

8. Run to Win

Sometimes life is referred to as a rat race, and it certainly is just that for millions or maybe even billions of people. That's no way to live. Life is, nevertheless, a race, but the difference in the world's rat race and the biblical race of life is that the rats never get anywhere. Nothing is accomplished in the end. The race that the Lord has for you is not just *run, run, run*, and then it's over. God's race is about the reward at the end.

Moses grew up as a young man who had everything this world could offer with no end in sight. However, Moses didn't live by sight but by faith! He looked with eyes of faith to the reward that comes at the end of the race. He could see God, who is invisible.

Hebrews 11:24–27 (KJV) says, "By faith Moses, when he was come to years, refused to be called the son of Pharaoh's daughter; Choosing rather to suffer affliction with the people of God, than to enjoy the pleasures of sin for a season; Esteeming the reproach of Christ greater riches than the treasures in Egypt: for he had respect unto the recompense of the reward. By faith he forsook Egypt, not fearing the wrath of the king: for he endured, as seeing him who is invisible."

You don't want to run this race of life just to run. You want to run to win! We are running for a crown, a reward that is imperishable.

The race is not about the race. It's about the reward, the prize at the end. You may see people running this race as though all there is in life is the race and then it's over. But remember the Word of the Lord. Surely, there is a hereafter. Run to win!

A Journal of My Journey for (Date)

_____

_____

_____

_____

_____

_____

_____

_____

_____

_____

_____

_____

_____

_____

_____

9. Your Source of Strength

Some days you may feel you have the strength of Samson, and other days may be more like you just got home from Delilah's barbershop! But it wasn't really about Samson's hair so much as it was his relationship with the Lord.

Judges 15:14 (KJV) says, "*And* when he [Samson] came unto Lehi, the Philistines shouted against him: and the spirit of the LORD came mightily upon him, and the cords that *were* upon his arms became as flax that was burnt with fire, and his bands loosed from off his hands" (emphasis added).

Judges 16:19 (KJV) says, "And she (Delilah) made him (Samson) sleep upon her knees; and she called for a man, and she caused him to shave off the seven locks of his head; and she began to afflict him, and his strength went from him."

So today's devotional could be called "A Tale of Two Samsons." In one scene we have a man who can slay a thousand Philistines with the jawbone of a donkey, and then the next thing you know he can't even shake himself free from Delilah.

What is the difference? What was the source of Samson's strength? What is the source of your strength? It's not your hair or your head or your heart or any other part of you. It's who you have living in you.

God is your strength, He fills you with joy. He makes you strong. His gentleness makes you great. It is important to remember that. Since your source of strength is from a source other than yourself, you must be *refueled* on a regular basis!

A Journal of My Journey for (Date)

_____

_____

_____

_____

_____

_____

_____

_____

_____

_____

_____

_____

_____

_____

10. Sitting with Jesus

As a Christian, it might seem like you should be exempt from all of the troubles and trials that nonbelievers face in this world, but it seems like there is plenty of trouble to go around! So what is the difference?

Matthew 5:45 (KJV) says, "That ye may be the children of your Father which is in heaven: for he maketh his sun to rise on the evil and on the good, and sendeth rain on the just and on the unjust."

But why do evil people get to enjoy God's sunrises? Because the goodness of God, if they receive it, leads them to salvation.

Romans 2:4 (KJV) says, "Or despisest thou the riches of his goodness and forbearance and longsuffering; not knowing that the goodness of God leadeth thee to repentance?"

So let's return to the matter at hand. What difference does it make if you are a believer or not if you still face challenges in this life? It all has to do with where you are sitting. What if you could have the best seat in the house every minute of every day? You can. As a child of the Most High, you do!

Jesus has the absolute best seat in the world. You could even say it is out of this world! But that's not all. God is so good and loving that He wants to share—with you.

Ephesians 2:4–6 (KJV) says, "But God, who is rich in mercy, for his great love wherewith he loved us, Even when we were dead in sins, hath quickened us together with Christ, ... And hath raised *us* up together, and made *us* sit together in heavenly *places* in Christ Jesus" (emphasis added).

Take your seat together with Jesus. Rejoice in the view from above and not beneath. Sitting with Jesus is out of this world!

A Journal of My Journey for (Date)

_____

_____

_____

_____

_____

_____

_____

_____

_____

_____

_____

_____

_____

_____

_____

_____

11. It Starts All Over Again

With winter all around and everything looking so dormant, it can get you to wondering about the purpose of a season that doesn't seem to get you anywhere. But of course, the Creator of all things has a reason for every season. Winter is a break from fall as well as a preparation for spring. When winter winds down, it makes way for spring, and it starts all over again. The same is true for each day. God created days to begin in the evening.

Genesis 1:1–5 (KJV) says,
In the beginning God created the heaven and the earth. And the earth was without form, and void; and darkness *was* upon the face of the deep. And the Spirit of God moved upon the face of the waters. And God said, Let there be light: and there was light. And God saw the light, that *it was* good: and God divided the light from the darkness. And God called the light Day, and the darkness he called Night. And the evening and the morning were the first day.

As it was with the first day, so it is with each day since. God divided the light from the darkness. There is the evening, and then we have darkness—a break from the day that has passed and a preparation for the morning of the next day. Why is this important? A couple of reasons present themselves.

First, it allows you to put the past in the past. Yesterday is history. You cannot press forward by looking back. And secondly, you can face the new day with a clean slate. This day can be the best day of your life filled with the goodness of the God who loves you!

Isaiah 50:4–5 (KJV) says, "The Lord GOD hath given me the tongue of the learned, that I should know how to speak a word in season to *him that is* weary: he wakeneth morning by morning, he wakeneth mine ear to hear as the learned. The Lord GOD hath opened mine ear, and I was not rebellious, neither turned away back" (emphasis added).

Every morning you can wake up to the Lord's presence and His Word speaking to you. Do not turn away. Acknowledge His voice. Even if yesterday wasn't exactly a perfect day and you were not the perfect child of God, you have a new day to do things God's way! It starts all over again.

A Journal of My Journey for (Date)

_____

_____

_____

_____

_____

_____

_____

_____

_____

_____

_____

_____

_____

_____

12. No Better Idea

These days it seems like everyone has a better way to do this or that, or they know more about it than you do. They have a more *progressive* way of looking at things or defining things. They feel they are more *enlightened,* and well, they feel they just know more than you about ... everything. So they say. But what does God say?

Daniel 12:4 (KJV) says, "But thou, O Daniel, shut up the words, and seal the book, *even* to the time of the end: many shall run to and fro, and knowledge shall be increased" (emphasis added).

That sounds familiar. Knowledge has increased. It has increased so much that most of what people *know* is nothing. They have been taught, and they think it is their opinion; however, as far as knowing, they know a whole lot of nothing!

First Corinthians 8:1–3 (KJV) says, "Now as touching things offered unto idols, we know that we all have knowledge. Knowledge puffeth up, but charity edifieth. And if any man think that he knoweth any thing, he knoweth nothing yet as he ought to know. But if any man love God, the same is known of him."

These know-nothings think they know how you should think and act, how you should raise your children and live your life. They think they have a better idea about what constitutes marriage and family. They even think they have a better idea about what a woman should do with the child growing in her womb.

Don't be intimidated by what is falsely called knowledge. There is no better idea. There is only God and His Word to guide every area of your life.

Proverbs 21:30 (KJV) says, "*There is* no wisdom nor understanding nor counsel against the LORD" (emphasis added).

There is a battle raging for your mind and the souls of the children. But you have the weapons to overcome all of those know-nothings with their so-called better ideas!

A Journal of My Journey for (Date)

_____

_____

_____

_____

_____

_____

_____

_____

_____

_____

_____

_____

_____

_____

_____

_____

13. A Foundation of Faith

The key to a building standing the test of time, weather, and other factors is to have a strong foundation. (Life happens after all!) It's like a tree. You see what is above the ground, but the secret to its ability to withstand all that comes its way lies beneath. There is actually as much of it below the ground as there is above! Again, the foundation could be likened to the beginning of any endeavor. If you start out right and stay on track, you will end up where you intended to be, but you can never expect to get somewhere if you don't start out in the right direction!

Second Corinthians 5:7 (KJV) says, "For we walk by faith, not by sight."

What does it mean to walk by faith? Faith is the foundation that holds you up every step you take, even if you are walking on water! It is the foundation that supports you when you don't think you can go on. It is your faith in the Lord Jesus Christ, the Word become flesh that leads you even when you do not understand His ways. It is the lamp for your feet and the light for your path. It is the foundation of faith that you stand on when you face Goliath and reach into that bag for a small stone to take down a big giant. It is the foundation of faith that gives you the words to speak when there is a mountain in the way that has to be removed. Faith, not sight, is the foundation of your life.

Hebrews 11:1–3 (KJV) says, "Now faith is the substance of things hoped for, the evidence of things not seen. For by it the elders obtained a good report. Through faith we understand that the worlds were framed by the word of God, so that things which are seen were not made of things which do appear."

Faith is the very substance of your life, the foundation on which it is built as a Christian. Just like everything in the natural world that you can see was made of things that you cannot see, so your life in this world is built upon, supported by, and nourished by what cannot be seen, even your faith.

Let faith be your foundation. Put your trust and hope in the Lord as you see God, who is unseen by the natural eye. See with eyes of faith. Walk by faith. In all your ways, acknowledge Him, and He will direct your path by faith!

A Journal of My Journey for (Date)

14. Right from Wrong

How can you tell right from wrong? After all, there are many voices clamoring for your attention. Words are powerful. That's what the Bible tells us.

Proverbs 18:21 (KJV) says, "Death and life *are* in the power of the tongue: and they that love it shall eat the fruit thereof" (emphasis added).

It is important that you speak words of life but also that you hear words of life and words of truth. The truth shall make you free, but the converse is also a reality. Lies will lead to bondage and eventually death.

Take a look at what happened when Eve listened to lies.

Genesis 3:1–6 (KJV) says,
Now the serpent was more subtle than any beast of the field which the LORD God had made. And he said unto the woman, Yea, hath God said, Ye shall not eat of every tree of the garden? And the woman said unto the serpent, We may eat of the fruit of the trees of the garden: But of the fruit of the tree which *is* in the midst of the garden, God hath said, Ye shall not eat of it, neither shall ye touch it, lest ye die. And the serpent said unto the woman, Ye shall not surely die: For God doth know that in the day ye eat thereof, then your eyes shall be opened, and ye shall be as gods, knowing good and evil. And when the woman saw that the tree *was* good for food, and that it *was* pleasant to the eyes, and a tree to be desired to make *one* wise, she took of the fruit thereof, and did eat, and gave also unto her husband with her; and he did eat. (emphasis added)

How is it that with just one conversation with the devil, Eve lost all sense of right and wrong? She began to see the tree differently than what she had previously seen. According to God's Word, she and Adam were forbidden to eat from that tree, but after a little pep talk from the devil, now all of a sudden she saw the tree differently. She saw it as good, pleasant, and desirable.

What should we learn from that experience? Look to God's Word as your only source of truth. Even if everyone around you is telling you one thing, if God is saying something different, choose God's way!

So let's get back to the question at hand. How can you tell right from wrong? If God said it, that settles it. The Word of the Lord is always right. Therefore, you can never go wrong with the Word. The truth shall make you free and always keep you on the right path

---

A Journal of My Journey for (Date)

15. God Is with You

There are many truths that we find in the Bible that can help us through each day, but among them we have this one that really stands out. God is with you.

How does this help? What can you gain from the knowledge of this particular truth? Let's have a look at a few things.

You are not alone. It helps when you face situations that can be daunting, even overwhelming, to know that God is with you.

Psalm 61:1–4 (KJV) says, "To the chief Musician upon Neginah, *A Psalm* of David. Hear my cry, O God; attend unto my prayer. From the end of the earth will I cry unto thee, when my heart is overwhelmed: lead me to the rock *that* is higher than I. For thou hast been a shelter for me, *and* a strong tower from the enemy. I will abide in thy tabernacle for ever: I will trust in the covert of thy wings. Selah" (emphasis added).

God is with you. In your weakness God is your strength! Joshua faced a situation that required a reminder of this truth. He had served the Lord faithfully by serving Moses, the servant of God. But then one day Moses was gone. It's easy in a time of loss to feel you are more alone than you really are. So here is what the Lord told Joshua and what He is telling you right now.

Joshua 1:8–9 (KJV) says, "This book of the law shall not depart out of thy mouth; but thou shalt meditate therein day and night, that thou mayest observe to do according to all that is written therein: for then thou shalt make thy way prosperous, and then thou shalt have good success. Have not I commanded thee? Be strong and of a good courage; be not afraid, neither be thou dismayed: for the LORD thy God *is* with thee whithersoever thou goest" (emphasis added).

What is the Lord saying to you right now? You have everything you need to succeed— all of the principles of prosperity. That's right, you have God's Word. Obey and be blessed. What else is He telling you? Be strong, God is with you. He is your strength. Be of good courage. You may not think you have the heart of a lion but in fact, you have something better. The lion of the tribe of Judah lives inside of you. God is with you.

Do not be afraid or dismayed, even with all of the uncertainties in the world. Trust in the truth. Walk by faith and not by sight. God is with you.

A Journal of My Journey for (Date)

_____

_____

_____

_____

_____

_____

_____

_____

_____

_____

_____

_____

_____

_____

_____

16. One Day at a Time

As you go through life there are certain events that stand out as being significant and a few things that are literally life-changing, but by and large, most days may seem like just another day.

It is important to remember that God does everything on purpose. He created time and the divisions of time for our sake, not His. He is eternal! When you look at divisions of time in the Bible, it is obvious that days are important. Even in the very beginning, God broke down the creation of all things into six days.

Just to get an idea of the importance of a day, let's look at a few numbers. Weeks are mentioned less than thirty times in the Bible, hours around a hundred times. Months do a bit better at more than three hundred times. There are almost a thousand references to years, but between days and nights, there are more than 2,700 references.

One thing you can take away from this little exercise is the importance of learning to take life one day at a time. God's provisions for your life are measured in days. It helps you stay dependent upon Him.

Exodus 16:4 (KJV) says, "Then said the LORD unto Moses, Behold, I will rain bread from heaven for you; and the people shall go out and gather a certain rate every day, that I may prove them, whether they will walk in my law, or no."

During those years in the wilderness, God provided food for His people. It didn't take them long to memorize the menu. "Let's see. Today I think we will have manna toast for breakfast. And for lunch we'll have a manna sandwich and then an afternoon snack of manna chips. And then for supper … manna burgers." They couldn't keep any for leftovers because they would spoil. Except for the extra day's supply for the Sabbath, manna had a one-day expiration date.

Psalm 68:19–20 (KJV) says, "Blessed *be* the Lord, *who* daily loadeth us *with benefits, even* the God of our salvation. Selah. *He that is* our God *is* the God of salvation; and unto GOD the Lord *belong* the issues from death" (emphasis added).

The Lord loads you down with benefits, but like the manna, there is an expiration date. Every day is a new day and a new load of blessings for that day. You can't save them up.

You have to keep your relationship with the Lord fresh and up to date. You don't want to face today with leftover manna. You need the fresh fire from the altar today!

This is the way to begin each day. You must depend on the Lord for His provision for today and not carry over any baggage (or wormy manna) from yesterday!

A Journal of My Journey for (Date)

_____

_____

_____

_____

_____

_____

_____

_____

_____

_____

_____

_____

_____

_____

_____

_____

17. Walk in the Light

We live in a world that is full of darkness because the ruler of this world is the prince of darkness. One day the devil will get his due, but in the meantime, you have the privilege of shining the light of the Lord in the midst of the darkness.

Matthew 5:16 (KJV) says, "Let your light so shine before men, that they may see your good works, and glorify your Father which is in heaven."

Every day you have opportunities to shine for Jesus. Where? When? How? Whenever you choose light over darkness, you bring glory to your Father. Live in the light. You are in the world but not of it. You are a part of the kingdom of light.

How can you live in the light? God's Word is a lamp to your feet and a light to your path. As long as you are walking according to the Word of God, you are walking in the light!

First John 1:5–7 (KJV) says, "This then is the message which we have heard of him, and declare unto you, that God is light, and in him is no darkness at all. If we say that we have fellowship with him, and walk in darkness, we lie, and do not the truth: But if we walk in the light, as he is in the light, we have fellowship one with another, and the blood of Jesus Christ his Son cleanseth us from all sin."

You are not in this world by accident. You have a purpose and a destiny. You are a part of God's special people. You are called by the Most High out of darkness and into His light.

Walk in His marvelous light and let it shine for all to see.

A Journal of My Journey for (Date)

_____

_____

_____

_____

_____

_____

_____

_____

_____

_____

_____

_____

_____

_____

18. Today Is the Day

What day? *The* day! The day for what? I don't know, but it's going to be good. If you don't know what, then how do you know it's going to be a good day? Because I know who!

Psalm 118:24 (KJV) says, "This *is* the day *which* the LORD hath made; we will rejoice and be glad in it" (emphasis added).

As you begin each day, there are a lot of things you do not know about that day. In fact, there is very little you know about a day before it has actually come and gone. There is only one who knows all about that day and every other. That is the God who created you!

So why would you rejoice and be glad in a day that you know almost nothing about? Because you know that God is good and merciful and that you can trust Him every minute of every day.

Psalm 34:8–10 (KJV) says, "O taste and see that the LORD *is* good: blessed *is* the man *that* trusteth in him. O fear the LORD, ye his saints: for *there is* no want to them that fear him. The young lions do lack, and suffer hunger: but they that seek the LORD shall not want any good *thing*" (emphasis added).

What are a few facts that you can glean about God from this passage? First, the Lord is good. Second, anyone who trusts in the Lord is blessed. That person will suffer no want and no lack.

Trust in the Lord and walk in His ways, and every day you can say with faith and confidence, "Today is the day. I will rejoice and be glad in this day, for it is made by my good, good Father."

A Journal of My Journey for (Date)

_____

_____

_____

_____

_____

_____

_____

_____

_____

_____

_____

_____

_____

_____

_____

_____

19. Don't Forget the Cross

Why is it important for us to remember the cross of our Lord Jesus Christ? Wouldn't it be more appealing to just concentrate on God's love and all of the neat things He wants to give you?

God is indeed love, and He does want to bless you with many wonderful things but all of this is moot if we are not *in* Christ. How do we get there? There's only one way, and that's through the cross!

Romans 5:6–8 (KJV) says, "For when we were yet without strength, in due time Christ died for the ungodly. For scarcely for a righteous man will one die: yet peradventure for a good man some would even dare to die. But God commendeth his love toward us, in that, while we were yet sinners, Christ died for us."

Jesus died for sinners. The only way to come to Christ is through the cross. It's not enough to just be sorry for past mistakes or to ignore them and play that they hopefully go away. Your sins won't just go away. They have to be taken away, and nothing can do that but the blood of Jesus that He shed on that cross.

Galatians 6:14 (KJV) says, "But God forbid that I should glory, save in the cross of our Lord Jesus Christ, by whom the world is crucified unto me, and I unto the world."

The Lord did not redeem you so that you could live your life for yourself but so that you could live your life for Him. When we are crucified to the world, then we can live for Him.

It would be easy (and a lot more comfortable and popular) to just concentrate on other things about Jesus and not really give much thought to the cross, but without the cross of Christ, there is no gospel of Christ.

The cross of Christ is the demonstration of God's love for you. It is the way to the Father.

What better way to face each new day than the sure knowledge that there is a God who loves you with an everlasting love, and the demonstration of that love is in the shape of a cross!

Don't forget the cross.

A Journal of My Journey for (Date)

_____

_____

_____

_____

_____

_____

_____

_____

_____

_____

_____

_____

_____

_____

_____

20. More than Wonderful

You may have heard of the seven wonders of the world, and now there are the new seven wonders and the seven wonders of America. And on and on it goes. Indeed, there are plenty of *wonderful* things in the world. God has given humankind wonderful abilities to build and to accomplish things.

Second Chronicles 2:1, 7–9 (KJV) says,
And Solomon determined to build an house for the name of the LORD, and an house for his kingdom. ... Send me now therefore a man cunning to work in gold, and in silver, and in brass, and in iron, and in purple, and crimson, and blue, and that can skill to grave with the cunning men that *are* with me in Judah and in Jerusalem, whom David my father did provide. Send me also cedar trees, fir trees, and algum trees, out of Lebanon: for I know that thy servants can skill to cut timber in Lebanon; and, behold, my servants *shall be* with thy servants, Even to prepare me timber in abundance: for the house which I am about to build *shall be* wonderful great. (emphasis added)

Let's look beyond the most wonderful things that have come from the hands of humans and consider for a moment some of that which has come from the hand of God. These things are more than wonderful!

Psalm 40:5 (KJV) says, "Many, O LORD my God, *are* thy wonderful works *which* thou hast done, and thy thoughts *which are* to us-ward: they cannot be reckoned up in order unto thee: *if* I would declare and speak *of them*, they are more than can be numbered" (emphasis added).

You cannot even count all of God's wonderful works, but here is just one to contemplate for His glory.

Psalm 139:13–16 (KJV) says,
For thou hast possessed my reins: thou hast covered me in my mother's womb. I will praise thee; for I am fearfully *and* wonderfully made: marvellous *are* thy works; and *that* my soul knoweth right well. My substance was not hid from thee, when I was made in secret, *and* curiously wrought in the lowest parts of the earth. Thine eyes did see my substance, yet being unperfect; and in thy book all *my members* were written, *which* in continuance were fashioned, when *as yet there was* none of them. (emphasis added)

As you enjoy all of the wonders of this world and all that God has done through the hands of humankind, do not miss out on that which is more than wonderful, fashioned by the very hands of God. We were fearfully and wonderfully made by God in the womb—the wonder of life, skillfully wrought by the Master and brought forth into this world for God's glory.

And this is just one of His more than wonderful works!

A Journal of My Journey for (Date)

_____

_____

_____

_____

_____

_____

_____

_____

_____

_____

_____

_____

_____

_____

21. What's Written in the Stars?

What's written in the stars? Nothing! Your future is not in the *hands* of the stars or the moon or the sun or the rocks or the trees or … well, you get the point. The stars do tell a story along with all of God's creation. What do they tell us?

Psalm 97:1–6 (KJV) says, "The LORD reigneth; let the earth rejoice; let the multitude of isles be glad *thereof*. Clouds and darkness *are* round about him: righteousness and judgment *are* the habitation of his throne. A fire goeth before him, and burneth up his enemies round about. His lightnings enlightened the world: the earth saw, and trembled. The hills melted like wax at the presence of the LORD, at the presence of the Lord of the whole earth. The heavens declare his righteousness, and all the people see his glory" (emphasis added).

When you see the lightning and feel the thunder, when you see the expanse of the heavens over the whole earth, you see His glory. Then you realize how small you are and how big your God is, and that's a good thing!

Psalm 19:1–6 (KJV) says,
To the chief Musician, A Psalm of David. The heavens declare the glory of God; and the firmament showeth his handiwork. Day unto day uttereth speech, and night unto night showeth knowledge. *There is* no speech nor language, *where* their voice is not heard. Their line is gone out through all the earth, and their words to the end of the world. In them hath he set a tabernacle for the sun, Which *is* as a bridegroom coming out of his chamber, *and* rejoiceth as a strong man to run a race. His going forth *is* from the end of the heaven, and his circuit unto the ends of it: and there is nothing hid from the heat thereof. (emphasis added)

So even though your future is not written in the stars, they do have a story to tell. All that God put in His firmament speaks to us—the sun by day (and quite often the moon will make an appearance during the day) and the moon and stars by night. Day unto day and night unto night, they speak to us. But what if it is not in a language we understand? Everyone understands this language. There is a God above the firmament who created all things and rules over all things. It would be utterly foolish to look at everything God has created and then turn around and say there is no God.

You will not find your future written the stars, but they are a constant reminder of the awesome power of your God, and when you see the stars above, you know that you are in good hands—His hands!

A Journal of My Journey for (Date)

22. Never Lose Hope

What is hope? In the Bible, we see the word used quite often. In the Greek, it means "to anticipate, usually with pleasure." It also means "expectation or confidence."

Once the apostle Paul was on a ship caught in a storm so severe that even the experienced sailors had given up all hope of being saved. But God had other plans and revealed to Paul that they would be saved.

Acts 27:22–25 (KJV) says, "And now I exhort you to be of good cheer: for there shall be no loss of *any man's* life among you, but of the ship. For there stood by me this night the angel of God, whose I am, and whom I serve, Saying, Fear not, Paul; thou must be brought before Caesar: and, lo, God hath given thee all them that sail with thee. Wherefore, sirs, be of good cheer: for I believe God, that it shall be even as it was told me" (emphasis added).

One thing that will keep you from losing hope is to always keep your hope centered on the Lord of all creation. Do not place your hope in the weather or the seaworthiness of the vessel or people or anything or anyone other than the Lord and His Word!

Psalm 31:24 (KJV) says, "Be of good courage, and he shall strengthen your heart, all ye that hope in the LORD."

When you trust in God, He will strengthen you and help you hold onto your hope! Be honest with the Lord, but don't stay cast down. Remember the victorious times you have experienced and the times you have seen firsthand the divine deliverance of the Most High.

This is where Abraham found himself when God made him a promise that seemed impossible. So in the natural world, Abraham had nothing to hope in—similar to Paul on that ship or how things may feel sometimes in your life. What did Abraham do? Contrary to hope, in hope he believed what God said to him, he did not waver at the promise of God through unbelief but was strengthened in faith.

Where does that leave you? Even if God's promises to you seem contrary to hope, you must believe in hope. Never lose hope.

A Journal of My Journey for (Date)

_____

_____

_____

_____

_____

_____

_____

_____

_____

_____

_____

_____

_____

_____

23. Restore the Joy

Sometimes life can get you down. How does that happen? What can we do about it? There are a few ways how that we can look at.

First, how is your relationship with the Lord? King David was a man after God's own heart, and yet he found himself in a dark place separated from the joy of the Lord. But he responded properly once he realized how he had blown it.

Psalm 51:7–12 (KJV) says, "Purge me with hyssop, and I shall be clean: wash me, and I shall be whiter than snow. Make me to hear joy and gladness; *that* the bones *which* thou hast broken may rejoice. Hide thy face from my sins, and blot out all mine iniquities. Create in me a clean heart, O God; and renew a right spirit within me. Cast me not away from thy presence; and take not thy holy spirit from me. Restore unto me the joy of thy salvation; and uphold me *with thy* free spirit" (emphasis added).

So if you find yourself in David's sandals, what can be done to get that joy back? Follow David's lead, confess and forsake the sin and cry out to God for His mercy. You will see your joy restored! The Lord is near to those who have a contrite heart.

Second, maybe you are just too busy to experience God's presence. If so, you are too busy! If you feel your level of joy is a bit low, it may be that you need to *practice the presence of God* more every day.

Psalm 16:11 (KJV) says, "Thou wilt show me the path of life: in thy presence *is* fulness of joy; at thy right hand *there are* pleasures for evermore" (emphasis added).

What can we do if this is the case? Make it a point every day to see the Creator at work in your life throughout the day. All of a sudden, you will experience the joy of the Lord.

Finally, you may just be going through one of those dark nights of the soul when it seems like the sun will never shine again, but it will be there when the morning comes. When you see the order of creation, it begins with the evening, and then the sun comes up. Things in this world got off to a rocky start with Adam's sin, but then Jesus came and made all things new. He came to restore the joy!

A Journal of My Journey for (Date)

_____

_____

_____

_____

_____

_____

_____

_____

_____

_____

_____

_____

_____

_____

24. Why Do I Have to Wait?

In this age when we can have everything in an instant, it's hard to imagine that there are some things that you actually have to wait for. Let's see. waiting for water to boil can be a tough one. In fact, some may tell that if you watch the water while waiting for it to boil, then it never will. But of course, you know that is not true. with the proper amount of heat, water will eventually boil. or you could just nuke it in the microwave, but then that wouldn't really be a very good lesson in waiting, now would it?

Anyway, back to the matter at hand. it's not that a watched pot never boils. It's that if every waking moment is spent thinking (and maybe even a little complaining thrown in for good measure) about the fact that the water is not yet boiling, it can seem like an eternity.

Furthermore, all that time and emotional energy was wasted concerning yourself with something that was inevitable. That water was eventually going to boil whether you worried and complained about it or not!

Ecclesiastes 3:11 (KJV) says, "He hath made every *thing* beautiful in his time: also he hath set the world in their heart, so that no man can find out the work that God maketh from the beginning to the end" (emphasis added).

God has a time for everything in your life. You can't see the whole picture, so you have to trust in God's timing and wait on Him. Better to have that water boil in God's good time! As a child is saying, "I can't wait to grow up," their parents are saying, "Slow down. Don't grow up so fast." The child just can't understand the parents' perspective, and so it is with the Lord's time for everything in your life.

Patience is the key to waiting. Why do you have to wait? God knows, but sometimes He isn't telling! Better to just trust in God's plan and His time even if you can't see any reason to wait. If He has promised it, you can count on it, and in His time, it will be beautiful!

Good things come to those who wait on the Lord. God's will in His time is beautiful.

Psalm 27:14 (KJV) says, "Wait on the LORD: be of good courage, and he shall strengthen thine heart: wait, I say, on the LORD."

Amen!

A Journal of My Journey for (Date)

_____

_____

_____

_____

_____

_____

_____

_____

_____

_____

_____

_____

_____

_____

25. The Next Step

Some steps are harder to take than others. When a child is first learning to walk, even one or two steps can be a major accomplishment. It's kind of a process. The boy needs to gets up on his feet. Then he realizes he is actually standing. *Wait*, he thinks to himself. *What am I doing? I don't know how to stand up.* And then comes the wobbling and toppling. Eventually, however, he takes one step and then two.

Sometimes life can make you feel like you are learning to walk all over again. You don't know what step to take next. Even if you see the next step, you may not know how to take it.

First, be sure you are taking the right step.

Psalm 37:23 (KJV) says, "The steps of a *good* man are ordered by the LORD: and he delighteth in his way" (emphasis added).

Be sure your steps are in line with God's Word. You can have confidence in your path when you know that the Lord of all creation delights in your way.

When you commit to walking according to the Word of God, you will always have an illuminated path before you and a lamp lighting each step. Beware of those who would try to lead you down a dark path no matter how sincere they seem.

Proverbs 4:19 (KJV) says, "The way of the wicked *is* as darkness: they know not at what they stumble" (emphasis added).

These can be well meaning people, but you can look at the fruit of their labors. By the fruit you will know them.

You can be sure that someone who is offended by the Word of God and by the name of Jesus is not going to be a good guide for your next step. That will lead you right into a ditch!

Ask the Lord right now, "Lord, uphold my steps in Your paths so that my footsteps may not slip." He will do it. You have His Word on it!

A Journal of My Journey for (Date)

_____

_____

_____

_____

_____

_____

_____

_____

_____

_____

_____

_____

_____

_____

26. Don't Worry

Those are two words that are easy enough to say, and you have probably heard them quite often throughout your life. You may have even heard a fish on a plaque hanging on a wall and singing, "Don't worry. Be happy," whenever someone walks by. We will cover the "be happy" part later, but for the moment, let's have a look at the part about not worrying.

It is not enough for someone to just tell you not to worry and not give you a reason not to worry. Wow, that was a lot of nots! In other words, it does not help you to not worry just knowing that you shouldn't worry. You must have something to base it on, a reason not to worry.

That reason is your loving heavenly Father.

Luke 12:22, 29–32 (KJV) says,
And he said unto his disciples, "Therefore I say unto you, Take no thought for your life, what ye shall eat; neither for the body, what ye shall put on … And seek not ye what ye shall eat, or what ye shall drink, neither be ye of doubtful mind. For all these things do the nations of the world seek after: and your Father knoweth that ye have need of these things. But rather seek ye the kingdom of God; and all these things shall be added unto you. Fear not, little flock; for it is your Father's good pleasure to give you the kingdom."

Any time you feel a bit of worry coming upon you, put it where it belongs—under your feet!

Fear, doubt, unbelief—these can open up the door to worry, but whenever any of them come knocking, don't answer the door! There are certainly plenty of things you could worry about, and if you run out of actual things to worry about, your imagination can provide a multitude of what-ifs to keep you worrying until the end of time.

The Lord knows the things in your life that could cause you to worry, and He does not expect you to pretend they do not exist. As always, He has the answer for you.

"Don't worry about anything; instead, pray about everything; tell God your needs, and don't forget to thank him for his answers. If you do this, you will experience God's peace, which is far more wonderful than the human mind can understand. His peace will keep your thoughts and your hearts quiet and at rest as you trust in Christ Jesus" (Philippians 4:6–7 TLB).

So what to do about all of those *things*? Pray to the Lord, tell God about your needs, and thank Him for the answer. Don't worry!

A Journal of My Journey for (Date)

27. Be Happy

Okay. Here is the second half of the refrain as performed by Billy Bass, the animatronic fish. The first part was "don't worry." And the second is "be happy!"

Just as you must have something on which to base your lack of worry, so must you have a foundation on which to build happiness. Just telling someone to *be happy* and not giving him or her anything to be happy about isn't going to work out too well.

So what do you have to be happy about? Is everything going just perfect in your life? Well, *everything* and *perfect* are rather strong terms to describe life in a world that is under the sway of the evil one (one of the names for the devil). Even if life is that perfect, it is not a foundation on which to build happiness.

First John 2:15–17 (KJV) says, "Love not the world, neither the things *that are* in the world. If any man love the world, the love of the Father is not in him. For all that *is* in the world, the lust of the flesh, and the lust of the eyes, and the pride of life, is not of the Father, but is of the world. And the world passeth away, and the lust thereof: but he that doeth the will of God abideth for ever" (emphasis added).

You would not want to base your happiness on things that are passing away, now would you? No matter how wonderful this life is, you do not want to hang your happiness on it. There has to be something deeper, more substantial, more ... permanent. There is!

Walk in the fear of the Lord and in obedience to His Word. It will be well with you, and you shall be happy—not because you have food to eat but because of the constant reminder of the faithfulness of God, who loves you and gives you your daily bread. That's really what the manna in the wilderness was all about. The Lord could have given each of His children a year's supply of food and left them with it, but instead He taught them to depend on Him for their daily bread.

The only way to be truly happy is to depend on the Lord God Almighty for your next meal, your next step, and your next breath!

Psalm 146:5–8 (KJV) says, "Happy *is he* that *hath* the God of Jacob for his help, whose hope *is* in the LORD his God: Which made heaven, and earth, the sea, and all that therein *is:* which keepeth truth for ever: Which executeth judgment for the oppressed: which giveth food to the hungry. The LORD looseth the prisoners: The

LORD openeth *the eyes of* the blind: the LORD raiseth them that are bowed down: the LORD loveth the righteous" (emphasis added).

When you have the God of Jacob to watch over you, every day is a happy day just like that first happy day, when Jesus washed your sins all away!

A Journal of My Journey for (Date)

_____

_____

_____

_____

_____

_____

_____

_____

_____

_____

_____

_____

_____

_____

_____

_____

28. Call and He Will Answer

If a tree falls in a forest and no one is around to hear it, does it make a sound? That is a philosophical thought experiment that raises questions regarding observation and knowledge of reality. So what is the answer? Of course it makes a sound just like all of the other sounds in the forest and everywhere else.

One of many problems with this so-called *philosophy* is the premise that we need to even consider such questions, and this approach implies that there are things like this that we need to figure out when we already have the answer provided for us plainly in the Word of God.

Colossians 2:8–10 (KJV) says, "Beware lest any man spoil you through philosophy and vain deceit, after the tradition of men, after the rudiments of the world, and not after Christ. For in him dwelleth all the fulness of the Godhead bodily. And ye are complete in him, which is the head of all principality and power."

This is the only time we find philosophy mentioned in the Bible, and alas, it is in the context of a warning! How could you be cheated by philosophy? If you even consider for a moment some of these false and deceitful ideas concerning knowledge, reality, and existence, you could find yourself feeling alone and forgotten in a world where *there is no one around to hear*. Praise God that is not the world we live in.

Psalm 139:7 (KJV) says, "Whither shall I go from thy spirit? or whither shall I flee from thy presence?"

And the answer? There is nowhere you can go from the presence of the Lord. God is everywhere. He is omnipresent. That means that wherever you are, there is always someone to hear you when you call out. You are never alone and forgotten even if everything you see and sense make you feel that way sometimes. Always remember the truth of God's Word, and don't let the philosophers of this age cheat you out of the blessing of His presence and the confidence of knowing you will always be heard by someone!

So let's skip the philosophy and get to the truth of the matter.

Psalm 34:17 (KJV) says, "*The righteous* cry, and the LORD heareth, and delivereth them out of all their troubles" (emphasis added).

Sometimes you may think, *The Lord doesn't want to hear from me again*, but that's not what He says. He does want to hear from you in order to deliver you.

Jeremiah 33:3 (KJV) says, "Call unto me, and I will answer thee, and show thee great and mighty things, which thou knowest not."

Don't you worry about what anyone says. You take God at His Word. Call to Him, and He will answer—even if you find yourself alone in the forest!

A Journal of My Journey for (Date)

_____

_____

_____

_____

_____

_____

_____

_____

_____

_____

_____

_____

_____

_____

29. What's on Your Mind?

Even if you are sitting still, your mind can be going a thousand miles an hour. But where is it heading? Where is it taking you? Obviously, if only your mind is moving, the rest of you will not be moving, at least not physically. Still, your mind and your thoughts can take you on quite the emotional roller coaster.

Why is this such a big deal? Many of the problems you will face in this life are actually *in your head*. It's not that you are necessarily imagining things, but it's more about what you allow to dominate your thoughts and the resulting emotions, words, and/ or actions. Things that you think about or the way that you think about things affect the areas of your life.

Psalm 19:14 (KJV) says, "Let the words of my mouth, and the meditation of my heart, be acceptable in thy sight, O LORD, my strength, and my redeemer."

Your soul includes your mind, your will, and your emotions. It's not just your words that affect your life. Your thoughts are just as important. Sometimes you may not even realize what's on your mind or what you are meditating on in your heart. Then all of a sudden, you feel a certain emotion, or you say some things and wonder either to yourself or maybe even out loud, *Where did that come from?*

So what's on your mind? If it is the Word of God and His law, then you will be blessed, fruitful, and prosperous. How can I be so sure? Because God said it, and if God said, it that settles the issue!

Philippians 4:8–9 (KJV) says, "Finally, brethren, whatsoever things are true, whatsoever things *are* honest, whatsoever things *are* just, whatsoever things *are* pure, whatsoever things *are* lovely, whatsoever things *are* of good report; if *there be* any virtue, and if *there be* any praise, think on these things. Those things, which ye have both learned, and received, and heard, and seen in me, do: and the God of peace shall be with you" (emphasis added).

Imagine how wonderful your life could be if everything that was on your mind was true, you never wasted even a moment thinking about the lies that are present throughout our society. All day every day, your mind was filled with noble things, just and pure, lovely and virtuous. For every situation in life, your mind was filled with positive thoughts—the report of the Lord! Imagine if you lived your life with a mind filled with the things that are worthy of praise to God. Wow!

What a wonderful way to go through life, if only that were possible.

There's good news. Not only is it possible, but that is how God wants you to live. What's on your mind?

___

A Journal of My Journey for (Date)

_____

_____

_____

_____

_____

_____

_____

_____

_____

_____

_____

_____

_____

_____

_____

_____

_____

30. Fear Not

Fear is defined as "an unpleasant and often strong emotion caused by the anticipation or awareness of danger." It is important to note that fear can be caused even by the anticipation of something bad or evil. How can you live a life free of fear when there is plenty of evil all around?

First, take time to listen to the words of your heavenly Father.

Isaiah 41:10 (KJV) says, "Fear thou not; for I *am* with thee: be not dismayed; for I *am* thy God: I will strengthen thee; yea, I will help thee; yea, I will uphold thee with the right hand of my righteousness" (emphasis added).

So maybe a little rhyme would be in order to help remember this truth. "Do not fear. Jesus is here." Or maybe tell yourself, "Why would I fear when my Jesus is right here?" Or you may want to go with the following: "When fear tries to come around, the name of Jesus will pull it down." Come up with something that you can hold on to.

The Lord has not brought you this far to let you drown! Think of how He has always brought you through every situation and fulfilled all of His great and precious promises. Put your trust in God and His faithfulness. He has called you by your name. You are His!

Psalm 56:3 (KJV) says, "What time I am afraid, I will trust in thee."

Why do we even need to be reminded of these things? Because sometimes fear will try to weasel its way into our soul. Look at the title of Psalm 56 and consider the place David was in when he wrote it.

Is David, the mighty giant slayer, giving us his secret to overcoming fear? That is exactly what you have here. You don't get the victory over fear by pretending like you never battle with being afraid. You get the victory by acknowledging your need for God's help and then giving the situation to Him (and letting go of it). In other words, put your trust in God, not in your ability to deal with the situation at hand.

"But how can I be sure I can trust God to bring me through after all the things I have done to let Him down?" It's not about your perfection. It's about His perfect love for you! Fear not.

A Journal of My Journey for (Date)

_____

_____

_____

_____

_____

_____

_____

_____

_____

_____

_____

_____

_____

_____

_____

_____

_____

31. Daily Bread

Matthew 6:11 (KJV) says, "Give us this day our daily bread."

What does it really take to physically survive in this world? You will need three things—oxygen (air), water, and food.

You could make it for only about three minutes without oxygen. (You could maybe last a few more minutes in the best of circumstances but certainly not much longer.) It's hard to realize that life is so fragile that we absolutely have to have an almost constant supply of something we can't even see.

What about water? You can go for about three days without water. In extreme cases you could maybe last a week, but you would be very thirsty by that time.

Okay, now we move to the big one—food. How long can you go without food? Depending on conditions, you can make it twenty-one days without food, but by that time, you would certainly be very hungry!

So to sum it up, you need all three every day. That takes care of your physical existence, but what about your spiritual well-being?

Genesis 2:7 (KJV) says, "And the LORD God formed man *of* the dust of the ground, and breathed into his nostrils the breath of life; and man became a living soul."

It would not be spiritually healthy to try to go more than a few minutes without breathing in the breath of life!

Revelation 22:17 (KJV) says, "And the Spirit and the bride say, Come. And let him that heareth say, Come. And let him that is athirst come. And whosoever will, let him take the water of life freely."

Sure, you can survive a few days without water, but you really need about ten glasses per day to be properly hydrated. Listen to the Lord when He calls to you and tells you to drink deeply of the water of life. Get in those ten glasses of life-giving water every day.

John 6:35 (KJV) says, "And Jesus said unto them, I am the bread of life: he that cometh to me shall never hunger; and he that believeth on me shall never thirst."

Okay then, what about food? Can't I be spiritually nourished if I get in a snack every month or so? Seriously? How would your physical body feel about that plan? Well, since some think about what they're going to have for supper while they're eating lunch, I don't think a monthly snack will go over very well.

There is a reason Jesus taught us to ask our Father for our daily bread. It's not just to have physical nourishment but rather to be nourished spiritually every day all throughout the day. Come to Jesus and be satisfied from above with that breath of life, the water of life, and the bread of life!

A Journal of My Journey for (Date)

32. The Shadow

Well, this title could call to mind different things. Maybe the radio program by the same name that ran from 1930 to 1954. No? Oh well, I guess that is so last century. But nevertheless, it just goes to show that superheroes come in all shapes and sizes.

Okay, it's time to shift gears. We are not talking about a 1930s superhero here. *The shadow* was around long before the invention of radio. We will have a look at the shadow of the almighty God. Actually, we are not going to look *at* it since it is not a thing, but we need a reminder of how to get there as it is actually a place.

Psalm 17:8 (KJV) says, "Keep me as the apple of the eye, hide me under the shadow of thy wings."

It is important to see the context King David gives us here. This is a prayer. David certainly went through his share of trials in his life and made plenty of mistakes. (Some of them were real doozies.) But through it all, he always knew there was a place where he could find refuge, where he could rest and quiet his soul. You can also make this your prayer for the God of David. His covenant of mercy is there for you today just as surely as he was there for David when he prayed this prayer.

Psalm 36:5–7 (KJV) says, "Thy mercy, O LORD, *is* in the heavens; *and* thy faithfulness *reacheth* unto the clouds. Thy righteousness *is* like the great mountains; thy judgments *are* a great deep: O LORD, thou preservest man and beast. How excellent *is* thy lovingkindness, O God! therefore the children of men put their trust under the shadow of thy wings" (emphasis added).

Psalm 63:7 (KJV) says, "Because thou hast been my help, therefore in the shadow of thy wings will I rejoice."

Here King David gives us a psalm when he was in the wilderness. How can you rejoice when you find yourself in the middle of a wilderness experience? Go to that place—the shadow!

Finally, we have Psalm 91:1–2 (KJV), which says, "He that dwelleth in the secret place of the most High shall abide under the shadow of the Almighty. I will say of the LORD, *He is* my refuge and my fortress: my God; in him will I trust" (emphasis added).

Who doesn't like a fortress, a castle with battlements and such? Well, God has just such a place for you, and inside that fortress rests the shadow!

A Journal of My Journey for (Date)

33. You Can Always Return

There is an old expression that says, "You can never go home again." There are, of course, variations on the theme, but the gist of it is that if you go back to where you were, things will be different. You will be different. That time has passed, and you can never go back. That's one of the important reasons that God gives you memories, and a filter to remember the good but not so much of the bad. The past is the past, and although you can never go back, you can always have the good parts of it with you!

If we can never go back, then why are there so many books and movies with time travel as a theme? Because everyone wishes it were so, and that adds up to a lot of book and ticket sales! Anyway, there is certainly no *portal* to go back and forth in time. We have covered the fact that time travel is out of the question (though still very much alive in our imagination). So how does that square with the second part of our theme for today?

You can never go back to a place in time, but you can always return to a place in a relationship when the Lord is involved. The Lord is with you, and He is in the restoration business.

Isaiah 44:21–22 (KJV) says, "Remember these, O Jacob and Israel; for thou *art* my servant: I have formed thee; thou *art* my servant: O Israel, thou shalt not be forgotten of me. I have blotted out, as a thick cloud, thy transgressions, and, as a cloud, thy sins: return unto me; for I have redeemed thee" (emphasis added).

No, you can't go back in time, but you can return to the place in your relationship with the Lord where He sees you white as snow, wrapped in a robe of righteousness because Jesus has become our righteousness.

Luke 15:11–13, 20 (KJV) says,
And he said, "A certain man had two sons: And the younger of them said to *his* father, Father, give me the portion of goods that falleth *to me*. And he divided unto them *his* living. And not many days after the younger son gathered all together, and took his journey into a far country, and there wasted his substance with riotous living. ... And he arose, and came to his father. But when he was yet a great way off, his father saw him, and had compassion, and ran, and fell on his neck, and kissed him." (emphasis added)

The prodigal son headed back home, but he knew that he could never go back in time—back to a simpler, more innocent time. But the lesson that Jesus is teaching us is that even though you can never go back to a place in time, you can always return to a place in your relationship when you let the Lord restore you. Love keeps no record of wrongs suffered. The Father is ready to run out and meet you and restore you. Don't allow your inability to travel back in time and change it to keep you from returning to the Father's open arms. He wants to see you restored.

A Journal of My Journey for (Date)

_____

_____

_____

_____

_____

_____

_____

_____

_____

_____

_____

_____

_____

_____

_____

_____

_____

34. Count Your Blessings

What kinds of things do you find yourself counting each day? Maybe during the course of your day, you are counting and adding up things relating to work or school. Maybe some of your counting has to do with keeping score.

Keeping score can fall into a couple of categories. You can keep score for a sporting event, and then there is keeping score in life, which is usually not so useful and can in fact be detrimental.

When it comes to counting in life, quite often it's like keeping score. You have a two-column tally. There are some things that you don't want to track or tally up because it will not accomplish anything beneficial in your life. For instance, keeping a running tally of the number of times someone has wronged or hurt you is not helpful.

Matthew 18:21–35 (KJV) says,
Then came Peter to him, and said, Lord, how oft shall my brother sin against me, and I forgive him? till seven times? Jesus saith unto him, "I say not unto thee, Until seven times: but, Until seventy times seven. Therefore is the kingdom of heaven likened unto a certain king, which would take account of his servants. And when he had begun to reckon, one was brought unto him, which owed him ten thousand talents. But forasmuch as he had not to pay, his lord commanded him to be sold, and his wife, and children, and all that he had, and payment to be made. The servant therefore fell down, and worshipped him, saying, Lord, have patience with me, and I will pay thee all. Then the lord of that servant was moved with compassion, and loosed him, and forgave him the debt. But the same servant went out, and found one of his fellowservants, which owed him an hundred pence: and he laid hands on him, and took *him* by the throat, saying, Pay me that thou owest. And his fellowservant fell down at his feet, and besought him, saying, Have patience with me, and I will pay thee all. And he would not: but went and cast him into prison, till he should pay the debt. So when his fellowservants saw what was done, they were very sorry, and came and told unto their lord all that was done. Then his lord, after that he had called him, said unto him, O thou wicked servant, I forgave thee all that debt, because thou desiredst me: Shouldest not thou also have had compassion on thy fellowservant, even as I had pity on thee? And his lord was wroth, and delivered him to the tormentors, till he should pay all that was due unto him. So likewise shall my heavenly Father do also unto you, if ye from your hearts forgive not every one his brother their trespasses." (emphasis added)

Don't count the wrong things. Count the right things! Count your blessings. Get your mind off of the things of this world and onto the things of God, and you will find yourself counting good things.

There will always be challenges in this life, but you will always have a choice. Don't concentrate on those challenges and enumerate them. Keep your mind on things above and count your blessings. You are loaded down with them every day. Don't let a day go by without counting. Like the children dropping their offering into the treasure chest at church, slowly dropping each individual coin, take the time to savor each of God's blessings in your life one by one. If you keep yourself busy by keeping a tally of all of the blessings, you won't have time to track your troubles!

A Journal of My Journey for (Date)

35. Responding to God's Presence

God is everywhere all of the time. He is omnipresent. Yet there are times when it seems like He may be everywhere else except where we are.

Psalm 10:1 (KJV) says, "Why standest thou afar off, O LORD? *why* hidest thou *thyself* in times of trouble?" (emphasis added).

The psalmist goes through virtually the entire book of Psalms describing how wicked people live on the earth like there is no God and they will never have to give an account to Him. Finally, he comes back to this at the end of the book of Psalms.

Psalm 10:17–18 (KJV) says, "LORD, thou hast heard the desire of the humble: thou wilt prepare their heart, thou wilt cause thine ear to hear: To judge the fatherless and the oppressed, that the man of the earth may no more oppress" (emphasis added).

Even though it may seem at times that the Lord is nowhere to be found, He is right there with you, even in the darkest of times. So how should you respond to the presence of the God of all creation? Let's look at Moses for a few moments. He understood the importance of God's presence. Let's see how it all got started.

Exodus 3:1–6 (KJV) says,
Now Moses kept the flock of Jethro his father in law, the priest of Midian: and he led the flock to the backside of the desert, and came to the mountain of God, *even* to Horeb. And the angel of the LORD appeared unto him in a flame of fire out of the midst of a bush: and he looked, and, behold, the bush burned with fire, and the bush *was* not consumed. And Moses said, I will now turn aside, and see this great sight, why the bush is not burnt. And when the LORD saw that he turned aside to see, God called unto him out of the midst of the bush, and said, Moses, Moses. And he said, Here *am* I. And he said, Draw not nigh hither: put off thy shoes from off thy feet, for the place whereon thou standest *is* holy ground. Moreover he said, I *am* the God of thy father, the God of Abraham, the God of Isaac, and the God of Jacob. And Moses hid his face; for he was afraid to look upon God. (emphasis added)

Moses responded to God's presence in humility, and that opened the door for him to experience more and more of God's presence as he continued to walk with the Lord.

The key to responding to God's presence is humility. When you humble yourself in the presence of the Lord and acknowledge His lordship over a situation even when you cannot see Him working or sense that He is aware of your situation, you will have a close encounter of the God kind before you know it!

A Journal of My Journey for (Date)

_____

_____

_____

_____

_____

_____

_____

_____

_____

_____

_____

_____

_____

_____

_____

36. Selfish or Selfless

One of the signs of the times is selfishness. It is very evident in our society today throughout the world.

Second Timothy 3:1–5 (KJV) says, "This know also, that in the last days perilous times shall come. For men shall be lovers of their own selves, covetous, boasters, proud, blasphemers, disobedient to parents, unthankful, unholy, Without natural affection, trucebreakers, false accusers, incontinent, fierce, despisers of those that are good, Traitors, heady, highminded, lovers of pleasures more than lovers of God; Having a form of godliness, but denying the power thereof: from such turn away."

But it is not unique to our day.

Judges 21:25 (KJV) says, "In those days *there was* no king in Israel: every man did *that which was* right in his own eyes" (emphasis added).

Since selfishness is the default for the flesh, what can we as Christians do to overcome selfishness and live selfless instead?

Proverbs 14:14 (KJV) says, "The backslider in heart shall be filled with his own ways: and a good man *shall be satisfied* from himself" (emphasis added).

Seek your satisfaction in this life from the Lord above and not from this world. What does it take to become that person?

Galatians 2:20 (KJV) says, "I am crucified with Christ: nevertheless I live; yet not I, but Christ liveth in me: and the life which I now live in the flesh I live by the faith of the Son of God, who loved me, and gave himself for me."

By faith in the Lord Jesus Christ, you can allow Him to live in you. You become a vessel, the temple of the Spirit of God. It requires a crucifixion. Before we can live for the Lord, we must be willing for our old man to go to the cross (and not come down alive). Then you can follow in His steps, and that will include selflessness because the self died on that cross with Jesus.

The key is not to just be emptied of self. Then you would just be, well ... empty! The key is less of you and more of the Lord. As you decrease, the Lord in you must increase so that you are filled to overflowing with Him.

A Journal of My Journey for (Date)

37. Do unto Others

There are certainly a few different ways that we could complete the sentence "Do unto others …" Let's try a few and see how they square with the Bible, shall we?

How about "Do unto others as they have done unto you?" That seems fair, doesn't it? But where does that get you? It might seem at the time that they had it coming, but in the end, nothing good comes out of it. You don't gain anything by responding to someone with the way they treated you. It just makes you like them. We want to follow in the footsteps of Jesus, not in the footsteps of someone who treats us poorly.

Proverbs 26:4 (KJV) says, "Answer not a fool according to his folly, lest thou also be like unto him."

Let's try this one on for size: "Do unto others before they do unto you." This has a little preemptive strike just for good measure. After all, you know how those people can be, so why not get a jump on things and stick it to them before they have a chance to strike first, right?

Now you're talking! Uh, no. What would Jesus do?

Jesus did not come into the world with the illusion that everyone was going to love him and treat Him as He should be treated. Jesus prays for Peter even as He is revealing to him that he will deny the Lord three times before that very night is over. This is what Jesus teaches us with His life, and this is what the Word teaches us.

Luke 6:31–36 (KJV) says
And as ye would that men should do to you, do ye also to them likewise. For if ye love them which love you, what thank have ye? for sinners also love those that love them. And if ye do good to them which do good to you, what thank have ye? for sinners also do even the same. And if ye lend *to them* of whom ye hope to receive, what thank have ye? for sinners also lend to sinners, to receive as much again. But love ye your enemies, and do good, and lend, hoping for nothing again; and your reward shall be great, and ye shall be the children of the Highest: for he is kind unto the unthankful and *to* the evil. Be ye therefore merciful, as your Father also is merciful. (emphasis added)

But what if they had it coming and you are just giving them their due? That's not your department. Give it to the Lord, and sooner or later, He will settle all accounts! Do unto others as Jesus has done unto you.

A Journal of My Journey for (Date)

38. Right or Wrong?

What's right? What's wrong? Who decides? What does it matter? Wow, that's a lot of questions, but we will get answers.

Proverbs 14:12 (KJV) says, "There is a way which seemeth right unto a man, but the end thereof *are* the ways of death" (emphasis added).

Just because something *seems* right, that doesn't make it right. That is an easy trap to fall into because we see things from our perspective, which is limited to … our perspective!

That is amazing to consider. Even if something *seems* right to every person on earth, if God does not agree, then every person on earth is wrong, and God is right.

So how can you tell right from wrong? You can by knowing the truth. You can by hearing and following one voice—the voice of the Good Shepherd.

The Word of God is the only source for truth. Jesus is even referred to as the Word. In God's Word, we have right and wrong laid out for us very clearly. In fact, just by taking the Ten Commandments and applying them to your everyday life, you will find yourself blessed beyond belief. God's Word never goes out of date. There is no expiration date on the Bible.

Just because we live in the twenty-first century, right and wrong have not changed one bit. God is eternal, and so is His definition of what is right and what is wrong. Yet in our day you see all around those who want to live like there is no God—no right, no wrong.

Isaiah 5:20–21 (KJV) says, "Woe unto them that call evil good, and good evil; that put darkness for light, and light for darkness; that put bitter for sweet, and sweet for bitter! Woe unto *them that are* wise in their own eyes, and prudent in their own sight!" (emphasis added).

The world puts down anything that is good and right as being bad, and the things the world celebrates as good are not just bad. They are awful.

That's what happens when you do not acknowledge Jesus as Lord and King. You start redefining right and wrong based on how you see it. Let God define right and wrong in your life, and it will be devil-stomping time!

A Journal of My Journey for (Date)

---

39. The Voice of the Master

The Lord Jesus calls to us as our Great Shepherd, and we are His sheep. We are to hear and only follow that voice. If we hear another voice, we are not to follow that voice but only the voice of the Master.

But how can we know it is His voice?

Second Timothy 2:11–13 (KJV) says, "*It is* a faithful saying: For if we be dead with *him,* we shall also live with *him:* If we suffer, we shall also reign with *him:* if we deny *him,* he also will deny us: If we believe not, *yet* he abideth faithful: he cannot deny himself" (emphasis added).

Our God never changes. He cannot deny who He is. He revealed Himself to Moses as the great I Am. He is not the God who was but is no longer. He is the God who was, who is, and who is to come!

The voice of the Master will never contradict the written Word of God.

Matthew 24:35 (KJV) says, "Heaven and earth shall pass away, but my words shall not pass away."

Listen to the voice of the Master as He speaks to you through His Word!

The Lord doesn't need an earthquake to speak to you (hopefully not). As long as you are listening for it, you will hear the voice of the Master. Every day throughout the day, the Master is speaking to you. Ask Him for ears to hear!

A Journal of My Journey for (Date)

_____

_____

_____

_____

_____

_____

_____

_____

_____

_____

_____

_____

_____

_____

_____

_____

40. Kings and Priests

Do you sometimes struggle with a sense of low self-worth? Maybe you sometimes feel like your life is rather insignificant. Every now and then, you need to take a step back and take stock of your life—who you are and what your life consists of.

Ephesians 2:12–13 (KJV) says, "That at that time ye were without Christ, being aliens from the commonwealth of Israel, and strangers from the covenants of promise, having no hope, and without God in the world: But now in Christ Jesus ye who sometimes were far off are made nigh by the blood of Christ."

When you look in the mirror, what you see and what God sees are two different things. It is easy for you to see the imperfect you who was once far off from God, but when the Lord sees you, He sees the blood of Christ, which cleanses you and makes you a new person.

It's like the song Wayne Watson recorded, which was adapted from a poem inspired by a sermon that is almost a hundred years old now titled "The Touch of the Master's Hand." The song is about an auction, and the last item to be auctioned is an old, dusty violin. So the auctioneer starts off with $1.00 just trying to get something for that old violin. But then an old gray-haired man makes his way to the front, takes the violin, dusts it off, tunes it up, and begins to play it. Suddenly, the auctioneer restarts the bidding but this time at $1,000! The crowd doesn't understand. How can something that is worth a dollar one minute be worth $1,000 the next? It was the touch of the Master's hand!

So if you look in that mirror and see a life that is worth a dollar, remember that God sees you through the precious blood of Jesus and that makes you priceless!

Revelation 1:5–6 (KJV) says, "And from Jesus Christ, *who is* the faithful witness, *and* the first begotten of the dead, and the prince of the kings of the earth. Unto him that loved us, and washed us from our sins in his own blood, And hath made us kings and priests unto God and his Father; to him *be* glory and dominion for ever and ever. Amen" (emphasis added).

Jesus is the ruler over the kings of the earth. He has loved you and washed away your sins with His own blood, and He has made you royalty. Hallelujah. It doesn't get any better than that.

It doesn't matter what you were. What matters is who you are. You are royalty. You are special. You have been called into God's marvelous light. You are the people of God. You are surrounded by the mercy of God.

A Journal of My Journey for (Date)

41. Ambassadors for Christ

An ambassador is "a diplomatic official of the highest rank, sent by one sovereign or state to another as its resident representative" and "an authorized messenger or representative." An important point relating to ambassadors is that they remain under the authority of their home country even while serving in a foreign land.

So how does that relate to your life as a Christian? I am glad you asked! Well, technically, you didn't ask. I posed a rhetorical question! Anyway, as a Christian, your home is in heaven.

John 14:1–6 (KJV) says,
Let not your heart be troubled: ye believe in God, believe also in me. In my Father's house are many mansions: if *it were* not *so,* I would have told you. I go to prepare a place for you. And if I go and prepare a place for you, I will come again, and receive you unto myself; that where I am, *there* ye may be also. And whither I go ye know, and the way ye know. Thomas saith unto him, Lord, we know not whither thou goest; and how can we know the way? Jesus saith unto him, I am the way, the truth, and the life: no man cometh unto the Father, but by me. (emphasis added)

If Jesus wants you to be with Him, then why are you still here in this world? Because He has a work for you to do—an assignment, a mission. But you might ask, "What about the fact that I have not been perfect my whole life? How can the Lord use me?"

First Thessalonians 2:4 (KJV) says, "But as we were allowed of God to be put in trust with the gospel, even so we speak; not as pleasing men, but God, which trieth our hearts."

The Lord wants people to be saved, and you have been approved by Him to be entrusted with the only thing that brings salvation to humankind—the gospel of Jesus Christ.

Ephesians 6:18–20 (KJV) says, "Praying always with all prayer and supplication in the Spirit, and watching thereunto with all perseverance and supplication for all saints; And for me, that utterance may be given unto me, that I may open my mouth boldly, to make known the mystery of the gospel, For which I am an ambassador in bonds: that therein I may speak boldly, as I ought to speak."

The apostle Paul was clearly an ambassador for Christ. If you want someone representing the kingdom of heaven here on earth, Paul is your man. But he has already gone home to his reward, his crown of righteousness. Paul has finished his race. So who does Jesus have to represent Him on earth today? Yes, you!

How can you be qualified to be an ambassador for Christ, the King of Kings and Lord of Lords? Because He became sin for you so that you could become the righteousness of God in Him; so it is time to get to work, ambassador. Represent and reconcile for your sovereign Lord.

A Journal of My Journey for (Date)

42. Priests of God

When you think of a priest, what comes to mind? To a large degree, the image that will come into your mind is based on your religious upbringing. If you grew up in a religion that includes priests, then that is probably the picture you are seeing right now.

Maybe you weren't raised in a religion that included priests, but you have probably seen some around. Either way, you may think of a person in long, flowing robes or maybe a white collar and a necklace of beads. By now, you probably have the picture.

Let's take a break and define our term. A priest is one who talks to God on behalf of the people.

Revelation 20:6 (KJV) says, "Blessed and holy *is* he that hath part in the first resurrection: on such the second death hath no power, but they shall be priests of God and of Christ, and shall reign with him a thousand years."

When you consider the definition of a priest, you see the position of ambassador taken to the next level. All those whose names are written in the Lamb's book are authorized to perform the sacred rites, not of a religion but of our God. You are a priest of God and of Jesus Christ.

Luke 10:17–20 (KJV) says,
And the seventy returned again with joy, saying, Lord, even the devils are subject unto us through thy name. And he said unto them, "I beheld Satan as lightning fall from heaven. Behold, I give unto you power to tread on serpents and scorpions, and over all the power of the enemy: and nothing shall by any means hurt you. Notwithstanding in this rejoice not, that the spirits are subject unto you; but rather rejoice, because your names are written in heaven."

Remember that in the very beginning, God told the devil that the seed of woman would crush his head? Well, you have the authority to crush the devil under your feet. You can stand in the gap for others against the devil because you are a priest of God. When you pray for someone, you are not just throwing words toward heaven. You are acting in your official capacity as a blood-bought servant of the Most High, and you have standing before God on behalf of others.

Revelation 1:5–6 (KJV) says, "And from Jesus Christ, *who is* the faithful witness, *and* the first begotten of the dead, and the prince of the kings of the earth. Unto him that loved us, and washed us from our sins in his own blood, And hath made us kings and priests unto God and his Father; to him *be* glory and dominion for ever and ever. Amen" (emphasis added).

Here is a prayer you could pray: "Father, I thank You that You have loved me and washed me from my sins by the blood of Jesus. And Father, I thank You that You have made me a priest unto You. I stand before You on behalf of my family and loved ones, and I acknowledge that I have authority from heaven on this earth over all of the power of the enemy in Jesus' name. Amen."

A Journal of My Journey for (Date)

43. The Sea of Forgetfulness

You have probably heard of the Red Sea, the Dead Sea, and the Sea of Galilee. And you *see* where we are heading today! But have you ever heard of the sea of forgetfulness? Maybe not since it isn't the official name for a body of water anywhere in the world but it does represent a very important truth.

There are plenty of things you need to remember every day, but there are some things that need to be forgotten and left behind as you move forward with God's plan. Let's have a look at this *sea*.

Micah 7:18–19 (KJV) says, "Who *is* a God like unto thee, that pardoneth iniquity, and passeth by the transgression of the remnant of his heritage? he retaineth not his anger for ever, because he delighteth *in* mercy. He will turn again, he will have compassion upon us; he will subdue our iniquities; and thou wilt cast all their sins into the depths of the sea" (emphasis added).

There you have it—the sea of forgetfulness! But how do you know the Lord won't go and drudge those sins back up again?

Psalm 103:10–12 (KJV) says, "He hath not dealt with us after our sins; nor rewarded us according to our iniquities. For as the heaven is high above the earth, *so* great is his mercy toward them that fear him. As far as the east is from the west, *so* far hath he removed our transgressions from us" (emphasis added).

Well, the east to the west is a long way apart, but still, the Lord could go and fetch those sins and bring them up again. He could, but He chooses not to because when He forgives, He forgets. Have you ever *forgiven* people for something only to bring it back up any time you want to get back at them? It's kind of like catching fish and stringing them up and putting them back in the water. Sure, they are in the water, but they are handy whenever you are ready to pull them out again.

Hebrews 8:12 (KJV) says, "For I will be merciful to their unrighteousness, and their sins and their iniquities will I remember no more."

The sea of forgetfulness is vital for you in two ways. First, where would you be if the Lord forgave you one day and then kept bringing your old sin back up every time you spent time with Him? And the second way is for dealing with wrongs you have suffered and are yet to suffer. By forgiving others the way God has forgiven you, you release yourself from the burden of unforgiveness and also make room for the Lord to deal with that person as He will. The wrath of humankind never accomplishes the righteousness of God.

Here's a prayer to put all of this into words: "Heavenly Father, I thank You for Your forgiveness when I confessed my sins to You and for the fact that You have put them in the sea of forgetfulness, never to be brought up again. Help me do the same with those who have wronged me—to forgive and forget. In Jesus' name. Amen."

A Journal of My Journey for (Date)

44. Time Marches On

"Time marches on" is a saying that basically means that whether we acknowledge it or not, time goes by nonetheless. It passes and is gone forever. "Where does the time go?" is another saying that usually comes up when the conversation turns to children growing up so fast or the length of time between visits with friends or relatives.

Psalm 39:5–7 (KJV) says, "Behold, thou hast made my days *as* an handbreadth; and mine age *is* as nothing before thee: verily every man at his best state *is* altogether vanity. Selah. Surely every man walketh in a vain show: surely they are disquieted in vain: he heapeth up *riches*, and knoweth not who shall gather them. And now, Lord, what wait I for? my hope *is* in thee" (emphasis added).

This is from a psalm of David. What is he telling us here? That life and time (for our present context) is like a vapor at best. It is not something that you can hold on to. It is transient, passing, and fleeting. You use it or lose it. It has an instantaneous expiration date on it. You don't have tomorrow's time to use today or even the next hour. You only have now.

"I wish it need not have happened in my time," said Frodo. "So do I," said Gandalf. "And so do all who live to see such times. But that is not for them to decide. All we have to decide is what to do with the time that is given us" (J. R. R. Tolkien, *The Fellowship of the Ring*).

We don't choose the time we live in. That is in the Lord's hands. But we do have a choice. We choose what to do with the time that has been entrusted to us. Time can either be spent or invested. If it is spent, then whatever we used that time on was hopefully worth it. If, on the other hand, time is invested, it will bring forth fruit from that investment, and if that time was well spent, it will keep making a difference in your life and in the lives of others.

Psalm 90:12 (KJV) says, "So teach *us* to number our days, that we may apply *our* hearts unto wisdom" (emphasis added).

Learning this truth will help you to make good use of the time entrusted to you. You must invest it rather than spend it.

Ephesians 5:15–17 (KJV) says, "See then that ye walk circumspectly, not as fools, but as wise, Redeeming the time, because the days are evil. Wherefore be ye not unwise, but understanding what the will of the Lord *is*" (emphasis added).

To *redeem* time here means to ransom time, to rescue it from being lost. If we are not wise, time can be lost, but if we understand what the will of the Lord is, we can invest our time in eternity!

"Father, help me to be a good steward of the time You have entrusted to me. Help me to be wise in the use of time and to invest time in eternal things and not spend it on things that are passing away. Teach me to number my days and make the most of each one of them. In Jesus' name. Amen."

A Journal of My Journey for (Date)

45. Choices

Unfortunately, the whole concept of choices and choosing has been, to a large degree, hijacked in our society by those who do not honor or fear God. You are left with the impression that even though you are supposed to be *tolerant* of everyone else, you are not free to choose what you think, feel, or believe. Rather you are to think, feel, and believe what you are told is right by the *collective*. You will most often find the word *choice* used is in act of killing babies, all of whom have no choice in the matter!

As always, we have to go to the only source of truth to sort this all out—the Word of God.

Genesis 3:6–13 (KJV) says,
And when the woman saw that the tree *was* good for food, and that it *was* pleasant to the eyes, and a tree to be desired to make *one* wise, she took of the fruit thereof, and did eat, and gave also unto her husband with her; and he did eat. And the eyes of them both were opened, and they knew that they *were* naked; and they sewed fig leaves together, and made themselves aprons. And they heard the voice of the LORD God walking in the garden in the cool of the day: and Adam and his wife hid themselves from the presence of the LORD God amongst the trees of the garden. And the LORD God called unto Adam, and said unto him, Where *art* thou? And he said, I heard thy voice in the garden, and I was afraid, because I *was* naked; and I hid myself. And he said, Who told thee that thou *wast* naked? Hast thou eaten of the tree, whereof I commanded thee that thou shouldest not eat? And the man said, The woman whom thou gavest *to be* with me, she gave me of the tree, and I did eat. And the LORD God said unto the woman, What *is* this *that* thou hast done? And the woman said, The serpent beguiled me, and I did eat. (emphasis added)

God created humankind in His image, and from the beginning of time, we have always had free will. That means we always have a choice. When confronted with his sin of disobedience to God, Adam blamed Eve. The Lord turned to Eve and confronted her, and she blamed the devil. Yep, she used the old "the devil made me do it" defense. News flash—it didn't work then, and it still doesn't work.

Life is all about choices. Your life to this point is the result of choices you have made, and your future will be determined by choices you will make.

Joshua 24:15 (KJV) says, "And if it seem evil unto you to serve the LORD, choose you this day whom ye will serve; whether the gods which your fathers served that *were* on the other side of the flood, or the gods of the Amorites, in whose land ye dwell: but as for me and my house, we will serve the LORD" (emphasis added).

"Father, help me not fall for the world's definition of choices. I choose You and Your Word, Your truth. As for me and my house, we will serve You, Lord! Help me to walk in truth in Jesus' name. Amen."

A Journal of My Journey for (Date)

46. Determining Your Future

So what does your future hold? To determine the answer to that question and to stay on target, you must get in touch with the one who holds your future—the God of all creation.

It doesn't matter what everyone else or anyone else chooses for their future. That should not be a factor in determining your future. Others' expectations of what your future should look like should not determine your future.

Isaiah 31:1 (KJV) says, "Woe to them that go down to Egypt for help; and stay on horses, and trust in chariots, because *they are* many; and in horsemen, because they are very strong; but they look not unto the Holy One of Israel, neither seek the LORD!" (emphasis added).

Don't look to this world or anyone in it to determine your future. Seek the Lord. He already has a plan for your life, and He knew all of your days before you were even formed in the womb!

Jeremiah 29:11–13 (KJV) says, "For I know the thoughts that I think toward you, saith the LORD, thoughts of peace, and not of evil, to give you an expected end. Then shall ye call upon me, and ye shall go and pray unto me, and I will hearken unto you. And ye shall seek me, and find *me,* when ye shall search for me with all your heart" (emphasis added).

You might say, "But there is not much the Lord can do with my future because of my past." Don't let your past dictate, determine, or direct your future. Never let the lies or past tricks of the enemy keep you from the future God has for you. Your past and future are two totally different things. You can't change the past, but you can put it where it belongs. And you can surely do something about your future. If you find yourself in a hole, quit digging! Decide right now that your future will not be based on your past.

First Corinthians 6:9–11 (KJV) says, "Know ye not that the unrighteous shall not inherit the kingdom of God? Be not deceived: neither fornicators, nor idolaters, nor adulterers, nor effeminate, nor abusers of themselves with mankind, Nor thieves, nor covetous, nor drunkards, nor revilers, nor extortioners, shall inherit the kingdom of God. And such were some of you: but ye are washed, but ye are sanctified, but ye are justified in the name of the Lord Jesus, and by the Spirit of our God."

Praise God for the washing, the sanctifying, the justifying work of our Lord Jesus Christ, and the power of the Spirit to wash us and keep us!

"Heavenly Father, I come before You right now not because I am worthy to be called Your child but because of Your grace. I have been washed from the sins of my past. I have been sanctified and cleansed by the power of the blood of Jesus and the Word of God, and I have been justified through Jesus' substitution when He took my place on that cross. I put my future in Your hands. Your will be done in my life. In Jesus' name. Amen."

A Journal of My Journey for (Date)

47. What Good Can Come Out of Suffering?

It seems like God, being a God of love and all, could prevent us from suffering, right? God did in fact create a world where humankind could have lived without suffering, but Adam, the first man, chose to disobey God.

Romans 5:12 (KJV) says, "Wherefore, as by one man sin entered into the world, and death by sin; and so death passed upon all men, for that all have sinned."

So here we are in a world full of sin … and suffering, but what about God's protection and deliverance as His children? The Lord delivers us daily from all kinds of suffering. We can live without fear in this world and experience righteousness, peace, and joy in the Holy Ghost. The joy of the Lord is our strength. God has given us a spirit of power and love as well as a sound mind. By the stripes of Jesus, we have been healed. These promises go on and on and on. Still, there is suffering in this life even for God's children. Let's start with Jesus.

Hebrews 2:9–10 (KJV) says, "But we see Jesus, who was made a little lower than the angels for the suffering of death, crowned with glory and honour; that he by the grace of God should taste death for every man. For it became him, for whom *are* all things, and by whom *are* all things, in bringing many sons unto glory, to make the captain of their salvation perfect through sufferings" (emphasis added).

Through sufferings, Jesus was made *perfect*, which means complete. Why did He need to suffer? After all, Jesus was already perfect? He needed to complete the work He came to do and to take our place. So if Jesus already suffered for us, why is there any left over for us?

When everything is going so perfectly in our lives that we don't seem to need the Lord, it might be easy to forget that we do need Him.

When you are suffering, the answer is the Lord, your deliverer. Ask God to show you things you could never learn during the easy times. Ask Him to bring forth the fruit of suffering in your life, and when His deliverance comes, don't forget to give Him the glory and the praise for delivering you!

Romans 8:14–18 (KJV) says,
For as many as are led by the Spirit of God, they are the sons of God. For ye have not received the spirit of bondage again to fear; but ye have received the Spirit of adoption, whereby we cry, Abba, Father. The Spirit itself beareth witness with our spirit, that we

are the children of God: And if children, then heirs; heirs of God, and joint-heirs with Christ; if so be that we suffer with *him,* that we may be also glorified together. For I reckon that the sufferings of this present time *are* not worthy *to be compared* with the glory which shall be revealed in us. (emphasis added)

"Father, help me to look to You as my deliverer in times of trouble, knowing that You will never allow me to go through more than I can bear and that You always provide the way of escape. Whether You choose to deliver me out of it or be with me through it, I will praise You and say, 'Lord You are good and Your mercy endures forever.' In Jesus' name. Amen."

A Journal of My Journey for (Date)

_____

_____

_____

_____

_____

_____

_____

_____

_____

_____

_____

_____

_____

_____

_____

48. Who Turned Out the Lights?

It seems that all around there is darkness in this world. Why is it like that when we know that God is able to do all things? He is omnipotent. Is He not able to turn the lights back on?

John 1:1–9 (KJV) says,
In the beginning was the Word, and the Word was with God, and the Word was God. The same was in the beginning with God. All things were made by him; and without him was not any thing made that was made. In him was life; and the life was the light of men. And the light shineth in darkness; and the darkness comprehended it not. There was a man sent from God, whose name *was* John. The same came for a witness, to bear witness of the Light, that all *men* through him might believe. He was not that Light, but *was sent* to bear witness of that Light. *That* was the true Light, which lighteth every man that cometh into the world. (emphasis added)

In verse 5 here, we see the word *comprehend*. Literally, the Word of God is revealing to us that darkness can never overtake light. In fact, darkness has no power. It is simply the absence of light. As soon as light comes onto the scene, the darkness has to flee!

So the place where you find darkness in the world is where the light is absent. If someone chooses to put God out of his or her life, then all that's left is … darkness. The same can happen to a nation if it chooses not to include the Lord. Then that nation is left in darkness. If a family decides that there is no place for the Lord around that family table, then you will find no lights on in that home! What about an educational system that kicks out God, His Word, and His Son? You can imagine what that would look like!

One night a Pharisee named Nicodemus (who was afraid of the light) came to see Jesus, and Jesus said, "For God so loved the world, that he gave his only begotten Son, that whosoever believeth in him should not perish, but have everlasting life" (John 3:16 KJV).

Have you ever noticed that one of the most well-known scriptures was spoken to a Pharisee when he went to see Jesus at night? Then Jesus finishes *answering* Nicodemus's unasked questions with the the following: "And this is the condemnation, that light is come into the world, and men loved darkness rather than light, because their deeds were evil. For every one that doeth evil hateth the light, neither cometh to the light, lest his deeds should be reproved. But he that doeth truth cometh to the light, that his deeds may be made manifest, that they are wrought in God" (John 3:19–21 KJV).

Whenever the gospel of Christ is preached, it's like turning on the lights. Trying to make people feel good about themselves in their sin is keeping them in darkness. Turn on the lights!

"Father, You have called me to be the light of the world. Yelp me every day to let my light shine before men so that they will glorify You. Help me not to hide my lamp but to let it shine for You in Jesus' name. Amen."

A Journal of My Journey for (Date)

49. Rejoice in the Lord

The word *rejoice* can be defined in the English language as "to feel or express great joy or happiness." And as we find it in the New Testament, the Greek word sometimes translated as *rejoice* carries the connotation of achieving victory over something. It's like you are joyful in spite of the circumstances you find yourself in. Quite often when you see the word *rejoice* in the New Testament, it is translated from the Greek word that means "to be cheerful, calmly happy." It was used very often as a salutation on meeting or parting similar to *cheers*.

So how does that help us? Let's have a look at a passage from the book of Romans.

Romans 5:1–2, 10–11 (KJV) says,
Therefore being justified by faith, we have peace with God through our Lord Jesus Christ: By whom also we have access by faith into this grace wherein we stand, and rejoice in hope of the glory of God ... For if, when we were enemies, we were reconciled to God by the death of his Son, much more, being reconciled, we shall be saved by his life. And not only *so,* but we also joy in God through our Lord Jesus Christ, by whom we have now received the atonement. (emphasis added)

Here we begin to see why we can rejoice in the Lord regardless of the circumstances around us. We have peace with God. We have grace from God to stand, and we have hope of the glory of God.

This leads to a life of rejoicing. As verse 11 says, you can rejoice in God through the Lord Jesus Christ.

Philippians 4:4 (KJV) says, "Rejoice in the Lord always: *and* again I say, Rejoice" (emphasis added).

Sometimes it helps if we are reminded to rejoice in the Lord. Do not worry about anything. Give it to the Lord in prayer, thanking Him for the answer before you even see the slightest indication that the answer is on the way.

"Father, help me today and every day to rejoice in You during the hard times as well as the easy times. Help me to remember that You are good all the time and that You know all things and that everything is going to be all right. I thank You for Your faithfulness and Your unending love for me. In Jesus' name. Amen."

A Journal of My Journey for (Date)

_____

_____

_____

_____

_____

_____

_____

_____

_____

_____

_____

_____

_____

_____

_____

_____

50. The Lord's Always on Time

It's good to be reminded every now and again (every day maybe) that our God is always on time. Of course, you and the Lord may not always be in the same *time zone*. After all, to the Lord, a thousand years is like a day! Wow. So it may not happen this century, even though I am waiting for the Lord to come through any minute? Fortunately, the Lord remembers that we are mere dust, and He sent His only begotten Son, Jesus, into time to make a way for us to one day spend eternity with Him. So the bottom line is that the Lord is always on time for our sake.

Galatians 4:4–5 (KJV) says, "But when the fulness of the time was come, God sent forth his Son, made of a woman, made under the law, To redeem them that were under the law, that we might receive the adoption of sons."

Ever since the garden of Eden, God promised that one day the seed of woman would crush Satan underfoot. Finally, just the right time came!

You might say, "But I have needs … right now. Why doesn't the Lord do something?"

Matthew 6:7–8 (KJV) says, "But when ye pray, use not vain repetitions, as the heathen *do:* for they think that they shall be heard for their much speaking. Be not ye therefore like unto them: for your Father knoweth what things ye have need of, before ye ask him" (emphasis added).

It is important to remember this spiritual truth. God is omniscient. He knows everything. Even before you ask Him, He knows what you need. Remember, ask and you shall receive.

But you may say again, "I am really struggling, and it doesn't seem like the Lord even cares. At any rate, He sure is taking His sweet time about helping me."

You must learn to trust not only in God's ability but also in His timing. There is a reason you cannot see and a purpose you cannot yet understand if something is taking longer than it seems like it should to come to pass.

Psalm 37:3 (KJV) says, "Trust in the LORD, and do good; *so* shalt thou dwell in the land, and verily thou shalt be fed" (emphasis added).

"Heavenly Father, help me to rest in You and feed on Your faithfulness. I know in my heart that You are always on time. It's just that I need a reminder sometimes. Help me Lord to have faith and to banish fear and doubt. In Jesus' name. Amen."

A Journal of My Journey for (Date)

---

51. It Might Not Be Easy

If anyone ever said that following Jesus was taking the easy way out or that if you accept Jesus as your Lord and Savior, everything will be sunshine and roses for the rest of your life or anything else along those lines, then they are definitely either mistaken, deceived, or just flat-out lying!

The fact of the matter is, of course, that there will be trials and tribulations in this life. Sometimes it might seem as if you are a trouble magnet. If you are not having enough problems for one day then a few more will find their way to you just for good measure. But that is not the case. Trouble is already around and doesn't need any attracting.

Matthew 6:34 (KJV) says, "Take therefore no thought for the morrow: for the morrow shall take thought for the things of itself. Sufficient unto the day *is* the evil thereof" (emphasis added).

If the Lord already knows there is going to be trouble, why doesn't He head it off at the pass?

John 16:33 (KJV) says, "These things I have spoken unto you, that in me ye might have peace. In the world ye shall have tribulation: but be of good cheer; I have overcome the world."

Cheer up. Jesus has already conquered the source of the trouble—the world. Life is about choices. Your life consists of the choices you have made and the ones you are making on a daily basis. Many times the choice will be between easy and right. Choose right!

Matthew 7:13–15 (KJV) says, "Enter ye in at the strait gate: for wide *is* the gate, and broad *is* the way, that leadeth to destruction, and many there be which go in thereat: Because strait *is* the gate, and narrow *is* the way, which leadeth unto life, and few there be that find it. Beware of false prophets, which come to you in sheep's clothing, but inwardly they are ravening wolves" (emphasis added).

Why did Jesus put in the part about the false prophets? Because then as now one of the most popular tactics of false prophets pretending to be sheep is to offer an easy way to heaven instead of the narrow and, yes, sometimes difficult, way that leads to life.

"Father, help me not to seek the easy way but the right way—the way that leads to life. Deliver me from wolves pretending to be sheep who would try to lead me astray and help me to see beyond this life to the reward that awaits. In Jesus' name. Amen."

It might not be easy, but it's right!

A Journal of My Journey for (Date)

52. Rest for Your Soul

In the beginning God created the heavens and the earth, and so it began. For six days God was at work creating everything. (Yes, that's right—literally six days.) Then He rested.

Genesis 2:1–3 (KJV) says, "Thus the heavens and the earth were finished, and all the host of them. And on the seventh day God ended his work which he had made; and he rested on the seventh day from all his work which he had made. And God blessed the seventh day, and sanctified it: because that in it he had rested from all his work which God created and made."

The need for physical rest is well documented. Of course, we don't need documents to tell us that. We have *the* document, the Bible. And we also require spiritual rest—the Sabbath.

Hebrews 4:9–11 (KJV) says, "There remaineth therefore a rest to the people of God. For he that is entered into his rest, he also hath ceased from his own works, as God *did* from his. Let us labour therefore to enter into that rest, lest any man fall after the same example of unbelief" (emphasis added).

When Jesus died on the cross for our sins, He cried out, "It is finished." The work of salvation was accomplished by Jesus on that cross. We must enter His rest and not try to work our own way into salvation. That is your spiritual rest.

But like our Creator, we are three parts in one—spirit, soul, and body. We have covered rest for the physical body. Spiritual rest occurs in the finished work of Jesus on the cross. But what about rest for your soul?

Jeremiah 6:16 (KJV) says, "Thus saith the LORD, Stand ye in the ways, and see, and ask for the old paths, where *is* the good way, and walk therein, and ye shall find rest for your souls" (emphasis added).

When you choose to walk in the way of the Word, you can rest in the Lord. Your mind and your emotions can be at peace.

Because of God's bountiful goodness toward you, you can set your mind at ease and rest your soul in His faithfulness and love.

"Father, help me to rest in You—not just spiritually resting in the finished work of Jesus but also resting my soul so that my mind and my emotions can be at peace and at rest, knowing that You are always watching over me and caring for me. Thank You for giving me rest for my soul in Jesus' name. Amen."

A Journal of My Journey for (Date)

53. How Late Is Too Late?

When you face a situation that seems like there is no way forward, it is easy to begin to feel like the Lord let you down. We will look at that type of situation and ask, "How late is too late?"

Mark 5:22–24 (KJV) says, "And, behold, there cometh one of the rulers of the synagogue, Jairus by name; and when he saw him, he fell at his feet, And besought him greatly, saying, My little daughter lieth at the point of death: *I pray thee,* come and lay thy hands on her, that she may be healed; and she shall live. And *Jesus* went with him; and much people followed him, and thronged him" (emphasis added).

Mark 5:35–42 (KJV) says,
While he yet spake, there came from the ruler of the synagogue's *house certain* which said, Thy daughter is dead: why troublest thou the Master any further? As soon as Jesus heard the word that was spoken, he saith unto the ruler of the synagogue, "Be not afraid, only believe." And he suffered no man to follow him, save Peter, and James, and John the brother of James. And he cometh to the house of the ruler of the synagogue, and seeth the tumult, and them that wept and wailed greatly. And when he was come in, he saith unto them, "Why make ye this ado, and weep? the damsel is not dead, but sleepeth." And they laughed him to scorn. But when he had put them all out, he taketh the father and the mother of the damsel, and them that were with him, and entereth in where the damsel was lying. And he took the damsel by the hand, and said unto her, "Talitha cumi," which is, being interpreted, "Damsel, I say unto thee, arise." And straightway the damsel arose, and walked; for she was *of the age* of twelve years. And they were astonished with a great astonishment. (emphasis added)

There are a couple of important things for us to consider here in answering the question at hand. First, you have to walk by faith, not fear. Second, you cannot look for confirmation from those around you as you may find ridicule instead of reinforcement. Get your strength to hold on from the Lord and His Word.

If you believe, you will see the glory of God! Pray through until you get the breakthrough.

"Heavenly Father, help me to have faith and pray and not lose heart, even if it seems too late for anything to change. Help me to pray through until I get the breakthrough. In Jesus' name. Amen."

A Journal of My Journey for (Date)

_____

_____

_____

_____

_____

_____

_____

_____

_____

_____

_____

_____

_____

_____

_____

54. Time for a Refreshing

One of the reasons God created times, seasons, evenings, and mornings is that He remembers that we are just dust, and as such, we need regular times of refreshing. Let's have a look at what it means to *refresh*. Refresh (*verb*) means "to give new strength or energy to; reinvigorate."

In other words, it means "to revitalize, revive, restore, fortify, enliven, perk up, stimulate, freshen, energize, exhilarate, reanimate, re-energize, wake up, revivify." (What does revivify even mean? It means to give new life or vigor to.)

Sounds like it may be time for a cup of coffee if you need that perk, right? Actually, we are going in a little different direction with this at the moment (although you may want to take a cup of coffee along with you on this journey). So let's look at the refreshing that can only come from the Lord and how you can be refreshed.

Acts 3:19–21 (KJV) says, "Repent ye therefore, and be converted, that your sins may be blotted out, when the times of refreshing shall come from the presence of the Lord; And he shall send Jesus Christ, which before was preached unto you: Whom the heaven must receive until the times of restitution of all things, which God hath spoken by the mouth of all his holy prophets since the world began."

Since the world began (about six thousand years ago when God created the heavens and the earth and all that is on the earth), God has been speaking of the restoration of all things and that day will come. But, until that time even the earth is groaning, waiting for its redemption from the curse. That means that all of God's children will have to struggle from time to time with a need for refreshing.

The first step to refreshing is repentance. This will release that heavy load of guilt and allow you to receive the refreshing that can only come from the presence of the Lord. Just taking time to be in God's presence is refreshing for your soul. It will revitalize you, revive you, and restore you. It will perk you up!

Psalm 19:7 (KJV) says, "The law of the LORD *is* perfect, converting the soul: the testimony of the LORD *is* sure, making wise the simple" (emphasis added).

So how can you get refreshed in the presence of the Lord? Where ever His Word is, there He is. Guess what the Hebrew word translated in this psalm as *converting* means?

It means *refreshing*. Spending time in the Word of God, which puts you in the presence of God, will bring refreshing to your soul. But how can you know when you need refreshing? Any time is a good time for a refreshing from the Lord.

"Father, I need You. I need a fresh touch from the Master's hand. I need to hear Your voice through Your Word as You speak to my heart. I need a refreshing, and I come to you in order to ask for a refreshing, for a fresh touch and a fresh anointing in Jesus' name. Amen."

A Journal of My Journey for (Date)

55. Life Goals

When setting goals, it is important to have not only short-term goals but some long-term ones as well, and you need some life goals too. It's like setting out on a journey and determining where you want to end up and then finding some markers or landmarks along the way just to be sure you are staying the course.

So how can you apply this analogy of a road trip to the journey of life? First, answer this question. Where do you want to end up when you come to the end of your journey? Most everyone would probably have a similar answer for that one. After all, it would be pretty foolish for someone to pretend like there is no God, right?

Psalm 14:1–2 (KJV) says, "To the chief Musician, *A Psalm* of David. The fool hath said in his heart, *There is* no God. They are corrupt, they have done abominable works, *there is* none that doeth good. The LORD looked down from heaven upon the children of men, to see if there were any that did understand, *and* seek God" (emphasis added).

The Lord is looking down from heaven. We're not talking about making a list and checking it twice. You'd better pay attention as there is going to be a test at the end.

Hebrews 9:27 (KJV) says, "And as it is appointed unto men once to die, but after this the judgment."

So what does all of this have to do with life goals? Since the answer to the first question is probably something like, "I want to end up in heaven at the end of my journey," then the next step is to be sure that all of your short- and long-term goals are taking you in that direction. In other words, if you set goals for your life without regard for God's will or if you put other factors ahead of your relationship with the Lord, you could find yourself veering off course.

Luke 12:15 (KJV) says, "And he said unto them, 'Take heed, and beware of covetousness: for a man's life consisteth not in the abundance of the things which he possesseth.'"

If you put God first in everything, you will be amazed at how He will bring things together in your life so much better than you ever could on your own. And the best part is that one day you will hear those words, "Well done, good and faithful servant. Enter into the joy of your Lord."

"Heavenly Father, help me to take stock of my goals and get them in line with what I want for my final destination—to end up in Your presence with a full reward. Give me the wisdom to discern those things that need to be reprioritized in my life and the grace to carry out my goals in Jesus' name. Amen."

A Journal of My Journey for (Date)

_____

_____

_____

_____

_____

_____

_____

_____

_____

_____

_____

_____

_____

_____

_____

_____

_____

56. Perfect Peace

It is amazing that peace is so hard to realize when it is something that you would think everyone would want in their lives. There's so much conflict and turmoil throughout the world. It seems that no one is immune.

Obviously, money can't buy peace. Some of the richest and most famous people in the world don't have any of it. It isn't something that comes with age and experience since both young and old can—and do—suffer from a lack of it.

What then is the answer? How can you experience perfect peace? If I can't have perfect peace, can I at least have a bit of great peace? Maybe I can have a little peace every now and then. Is that too much to ask? Fortunately, all that is possible!

Psalm 29:11 (KJV) says, "The LORD will give strength unto his people; the LORD will bless his people with peace."

The first thing, which many overlook, is that the blessing of peace along with all of the blessings enumerated in the Word of God pertaining to "His people." It seems like everyone wants the blessings that come with being Christian, but some never consider that you must first become a Christian to receive the blessings God has promised to "His people." If you have received Jesus Christ as your Lord and Savior, then this promise is for you—the promise of peace.

Psalm 119:165 (KJV) says, "Great peace have they which love thy law: and nothing shall offend them."

Second, remember that you have been given God's Word. This is literally the Word of God written and forever settled in heaven. You do not have to live in an uncertain world with an uncertain future full of questions with no answers. You can live a life of great peace because you know what the God of creation has already said about you and has already provided for you!

Philippians 4:6–7 (KJV) says, "Be careful for nothing; but in every thing by prayer and supplication with thanksgiving let your requests be made known unto God. And the peace of God, which passeth all understanding, shall keep your hearts and minds through Christ Jesus."

This peace is so great it surpasses all understanding. When you take God at His Word, His peace takes over your heart and soul. That is great!

Isaiah 26:3(KJV) says, "Thou wilt keep *him* in perfect peace, *whose* mind *is* stayed *on thee:* because he trusteth in thee." (emphasis added).

Finally, perfect peace can only come from a perfect God. When you trust in the Lord and keep your mind set on Him, you will find that He is able to keep you in His perfect peace!

"Heavenly Father, right now I choose to trust You and Your Word. I ask for and receive by faith Your peace, which passes all understanding. That is at this very moment guarding my heart and mind and keeping me in perfect peace. In Jesus' name. Amen."

A Journal of My Journey for (Date)

57. The Two Great Commandments

Matthew 22:36 (KJV) says, "Master, which *is* the great commandment in the law? Jesus said unto him, Thou shalt love the Lord thy God with all thy heart, and with all thy soul, and with all thy mind. This is the first and great commandment. And the second *is* like unto it, Thou shalt love thy neighbour as thyself. On these two commandments hang all the law and the prophets" (emphasis added).

If you had Jesus right here with you (though He is in fact right here with you in spirit) and you were able to ask just one question, what would it be? There are plenty of things that would probably come to mind, and many of them would more than likely be specific to your life or those that you love. Furthermore, it is highly likely that your one question would begin with the word *why*. That word is popular even for very little ones. It seems as soon as children learn to speak, this becomes one of the first words in their vocabulary and for good reason. Coming before the Lord as children, we have plenty of why questions that we would like to ask.

But the question in our scripture begins with another word—*which*. Indeed, it is a question well worth hearing the answer to, so let's see what Jesus has to say. Being a Jew, Jesus knew immediately the correct answer taken from Deuteronomy. *You shall love the Lord your God*. But what does that mean? He goes on to clarify. How can you love God with all of your heart, your soul, and your mind?

Consider this: What is the most important thing to you in the whole world? That's where your heart is. What occupies your emotions and your thoughts? That's where your soul and mind are. So Jesus should be at the center of everything in my life? Yes. He should be the most important thing in your life above all else.

Even though there was only one question, Jesus' answer comes in two parts. Not only is Jesus to have first place in your life, but you should also consider others. When you obey the greatest commandments, you are in fact keeping with the spirit of the entire law of Moses.

If you want to live a life that you can be sure is pleasing to God, here is the *answer* you are looking for.

"Heavenly Father, I want to be pleasing to You and reflect Your love to others. I know I cannot love others until I first fully love You, putting You first in all things. I acknowledge You as not only Savior but also Lord of all things in my life. Help me to love You with all of my heart, soul, and mind. In Jesus' name. Amen."

A Journal of My Journey for (Date)

58. The Benefits of Being the Lord's Sheep

Psalm 68:19 (KJV) says, "Blessed *be* the Lord, *who* daily loadeth us *with benefits, even* the God of our salvation. Selah" (emphasis added).

It is great to know that our God not only provides us with a home in heaven but is also loading us down daily with blessings today! The key is to acknowledge the Lord in all of your ways and put your trust in Him.

Psalm 23 (KJV) says,
The LORD *is* my shepherd; I shall not want. He maketh me to lie down in green pastures: he leadeth me beside the still waters. He restoreth my soul: he leadeth me in the paths of righteousness for his name's sake. Yea, though I walk through the valley of the shadow of death, I will fear no evil: for thou *art* with me; thy rod and thy staff they comfort me. Thou preparest a table before me in the presence of mine enemies: thou anointest my head with oil; my cup runneth over. Surely goodness and mercy shall follow me all the days of my life: and I will dwell in the house of the LORD for ever.

There's enough truth in this psalm to keep a child of God rejoicing for the rest of his or her life. Let's enumerate a few of the daily benefits of being the Lord's sheep.

"I shall not want." Wow. That alone is enough to keep you going every day; God's provision for every area of your life every day.

"green pastures" If you are lying down with all of that food around you, it means that you have already had your fill and you are ready for an afternoon nap. You have more than enough!

"still waters" Deep, still waters signify all that you need to satisfy your thirst and to bring forth fruitfulness.

"He restores" implies the daily provision of restoration. You know how sheep can get themselves into a wooly mess sometimes!

"He leads." Our God doesn't just tell us which way to go. He leads the way, and we are never alone. He will never leave us or forsake us.

"I will fear no evil." As long as the Good Shepherd is with us, we have no need to fear, even in times when there is darkness all around us. In the darkest times, God's light shines brightest!

"Your rod and Your staff." It is a comfort to know that the Lord is always there to correct and to deliver. Through the Lord's discipline, we grow.

"You prepare a table." What a picture of victorious peace to be able to sit down and enjoy the blessings of God even in the midst of your enemies all around.

"You anoint my head." When you get bruised and scraped in battle, the Good Shepherd is ready with the anointing oil to bring comfort and healing.

"My cup runs over." That sums up the daily life of the Lord's sheep—blessings that cannot be contained.

"Goodness, mercy and forever blessings." That is the life your Father intends for you. As you live the life of a sheep in His flock, goodness and mercy follow you around every day, and your cup of blessing is running over. Even those around you get a little bit of that blessing on them. You are comforted and restored and filled and refreshed and ... just plain blessed.

A Journal of My Journey for (Date)

59. The Race of Life

Life is like a race that we are running. For many people it is more like a rat race. What is the purpose of a rat running on a wheel that is getting him nowhere? Exactly. There is no purpose. Those who live their lives pursuing things that they will leave behind when the race is over are running the wrong kind of race!

First Corinthians 9:24–27 (KJV) says,
Know ye not that they which run in a race run all, but one receiveth the prize? So run, that ye may obtain. And every man that striveth for the mastery is temperate in all things. Now they *do it* to obtain a corruptible crown; but we an incorruptible. I therefore so run, not as uncertainly; so fight I, not as one that beateth the air: But I keep under my body, and bring *it* into subjection: lest that by any means, when I have preached to others, I myself should be a castaway. (emphasis added)

It is not so much that you are running against anyone or anything but rather that you are running toward something—to obtain the prize, the crown of life.

Hebrews 12:1–3 (KJV) says,
Wherefore seeing we also are compassed about with so great a cloud of witnesses, let us lay aside every weight, and the sin which doth so easily beset *us,* and let us run with patience the race that is set before us, Looking unto Jesus the author and finisher of *our* faith; who for the joy that was set before him endured the cross, despising the shame, and is set down at the right hand of the throne of God. For consider him that endured such contradiction of sinners against himself, lest ye be wearied and faint in your minds. (emphasis added)

This race is not a sprint. The prize doesn't go to the swiftest runner. This is a race that calls for endurance. Many times you may get weary in the race, but you have to keep pressing forward. When you grow weary, get refreshed in the presence of God and run on!

Isaiah :28–31 (KJV) says,
Hast thou not known? hast thou not heard, *that* the everlasting God, the LORD, the Creator of the ends of the earth, fainteth not, neither is weary? *there is* no searching of his understanding. He giveth power to the faint; and to *them that have* no might he increaseth strength. Even the youths shall faint and be weary, and the young men shall utterly fall: But they that wait upon the LORD shall renew *their* strength; they shall

mount up with wings as eagles; they shall run, and not be weary; *and* they shall walk, and not faint. (emphasis added)

Just because you grow weary sometimes, that does not mean you are not strong. It just means you need to be refueled by the Creator of the earth.

"Heavenly Father, I want to run for the prize so that I may gain Christ and heaven. Give me the strength, and when I have no strength, renew my strength to run with endurance in this race of life that You have for me. In Jesus' name. Amen."

A Journal of My Journey for (Date)

60. Saints and Sinners

Most people probably have a good idea of what a sinner is. That would be pretty much everybody, right? After all, nobody's perfect. That is true. All have sinned, so the sinners column would include literally everyone.

Romans 3:10–12 (KJV) says, "As it is written, There is none righteous, no, not one: There is none that understandeth, there is none that seeketh after God. They are all gone out of the way, they are together become unprofitable; there is none that doeth good, no, not one."

Romans 3:23 (KJV) says, "For all have sinned, and come short of the glory of God."

Well, that seems pretty straightforward. We are all just a bunch of sinners. So where do the saints come in? If everyone who has ever lived is a sinner, there's no one left to be a saint, right?

First Timothy 1:15–17 (KJV) says, "This *is* a faithful saying, and worthy of all acceptation, that Christ Jesus came into the world to save sinners; of whom I am chief. Howbeit for this cause I obtained mercy, that in me first Jesus Christ might show forth all longsuffering, for a pattern to them which should hereafter believe on him to life everlasting. Now unto the King eternal, immortal, invisible, the only wise God, *be* honour and glory for ever and ever. Amen" (emphasis added).

The apostle Paul refers to himself as the chief of sinners. Wow! If anyone should have risen to sainthood level, you would think it would have been Paul. But how can someone be a saint and a sinner?

Second Corinthians 5:16–19 (KJV) says,
Wherefore henceforth know we no man after the flesh: yea, though we have known Christ after the flesh, yet now henceforth know we *him* no more. Therefore if any man *be* in Christ, *he is* a new creature: old things are passed away; behold, all things are become new. And all things *are* of God, who hath reconciled us to himself by Jesus Christ, and hath given to us the ministry of reconciliation; To wit, that God was in Christ, reconciling the world unto himself, not imputing their trespasses unto them; and hath committed unto us the word of reconciliation. (emphasis added)

Once you have your sins washed away by the blood of Jesus, the Father does not see you as a sinner. He sees you as a saint!

First Corinthians 1:2–3 (KJV) says, "Unto the church of God which is at Corinth, to them that are sanctified in Christ Jesus, called *to be* saints, with all that in every place call upon the name of Jesus Christ our Lord, both theirs and ours: Grace *be* unto you, and peace, from God our Father, and *from* the Lord Jesus Christ" (emphasis added).

God did not call you to be a sinner. That comes naturally. He called you to be a saint!

A Journal of My Journey for (Date)

_____

_____

_____

_____

_____

_____

_____

_____

_____

_____

_____

_____

_____

_____

_____

_____

_____

_____

61. Mourning into Dancing

How can a bad day be turned into a good day? What makes a day good or bad anyway? To answer these questions and to get a better understanding of life in general, it is important to separate the constants in life from the inconsistent things (i.e., the things that never change from the things that are constantly changing).

Psalm 30:11–12 (KJV) says, "Thou hast turned for me my mourning into dancing: thou hast put off my sackcloth, and girded me with gladness; To the end that *my* glory may sing praise to thee, and not be silent. O LORD my God, I will give thanks unto thee for ever" (emphasis added).

The key word that we find used four times in the previous passage is *you*. The Lord is the constant in your life. Everything else may change around you, but the Lord stays the same. This is what makes a good day good. It's God!

Even though other factors in your life may be getting you down, you can always get a pick-me-up from the Lord. He will never let you down, and if you are down, He will always pick you up—if you let Him.

Psalm 37:3–5 (KJV) says, "Trust in the LORD, and do good; *so* shalt thou dwell in the land, and verily thou shalt be fed. Delight thyself also in the LORD; and he shall give thee the desires of thine heart. Commit thy way unto the LORD; trust also in him; and he shall bring *it* to pass" (emphasis added).

How can you let the Lord pick you up and turn your day right around? Here are a few clues from the previous scripture.
Trust in the Lord.
Obey the Lord. (Do good.)
Stick close to the Lord. (Dwell in God.)
Meditate on God's faithfulness.
Find your delight in the Lord.
Commit your way to the Lord. Lay it all before Him.
Trust Him. When you lay it down at the feet of Jesus, don't pick it back up again!
The Lord will always come through.

"Heavenly Father, help me to lay everything at the feet of my Lord, Jesus Christ, and trust You to take care of me. I know You will pick me up and turn my day around, and I trust You with this day in Jesus' name. Amen."

A Journal of My Journey for (Date)

62. A Good Time for Trusting

Psalm 56:3 (KJV) says, "What time I am afraid, I will trust in thee."

When we read these words, a couple of responses spring to mind. There is the super spiritual approach, which would ask, "What's wrong with these people? If they are God's children, why would they ever be afraid?" And then there's the Christian who may respond, "Amen. Sometimes I am afraid, but I still love God and trust Him. I just need to be reminded of these things sometimes."

So what came to your mind when you read this verse? Did you wonder what kind of a person felt this way? King David wrote this Psalm and here are the explanatory notes for this Psalm: To the Chief Musician; set to [the tune of] "Silent Dove Among Those Far Away" A Mikhtam of David [A record of memorable thoughts] when the Philistines seized him in Gath.

Hold on a minute. How could these be some of King David's *memorable thoughts*? Isn't David the one who, as a young man, faced the mighty Goliath? When all of the armies of Israel were shaking in their sandals, the young shepherd boy ran into the battle and boldly proclaimed victory to the giant's face. Many people sang, "Saul has slain his thousands, but David his tens of thousands".

That is the very same David—the sweet singer of Israel, the man after God's own heart. But sometimes he was afraid, but that's okay. David knew what to do during those times. It is a choice. It is a stand. It is a proclamation. "I will trust in You."

"Father, help me during those times when I am afraid to trust in You. I acknowledge Your faithfulness and Your steadfast love and care for me in Jesus' name. Amen."

A Journal of My Journey for (Date)

_____

_____

_____

_____

_____

_____

_____

_____

_____

_____

_____

_____

_____

_____

_____

63. Things to Consider

Luke 12:22–32 (KJV) says,

And he said unto his disciples, Therefore I say unto you, Take no thought for your life, what ye shall eat; neither for the body, what ye shall put on. The life is more than meat, and the body *is more* than raiment. Consider the ravens: for they neither sow nor reap; which neither have storehouse nor barn; and God feedeth them: how much more are ye better than the fowls? And which of you with taking thought can add to his stature one cubit? If ye then be not able to do that thing which is least, why take ye thought for the rest? Consider the lilies how they grow: they toil not, they spin not; and yet I say unto you, that Solomon in all his glory was not arrayed like one of these. If then God so clothe the grass, which is to day in the field, and to morrow is cast into the oven; how much more *will he clothe* you, O ye of little faith? And seek not ye what ye shall eat, or what ye shall drink, neither be ye of doubtful mind. For all these things do the nations of the world seek after: and your Father knoweth that ye have need of these things. But rather seek ye the kingdom of God; and all these things shall be added unto you. Fear not, little flock; for it is your Father's good pleasure to give you the kingdom. (emphasis added)

Do you take time each day to consider the birds of the air or the flowers of the field? What an awesome provider your heavenly Father is! Solomon was the richest man in the world, and yet all of that wealth could not buy him a wardrobe that matched the lilies.

If you sometimes battle with worry, remember that one way to treat an anxious mind is to consider the things you see all around you that reveal God's glory. All of the natural world goes through each day without one bit of worry. The birds sing their song, and the flowers reach up toward their heavenly provider and burst forth in a magnificent array of colors.

But you still need to eat, right, and at least something to wear? Have you ever looked into a pantry seemingly full of food and not see anything to eat? What about a closet full of clothes but nothing to wear? It happens! Yes, you need food and clothing and all of the things that it takes in this world to live each day. The good news is that your heavenly Father knows you need these things, and it is His good pleasure to provide everything you need when you seek Him and His kingdom.

A Journal of My Journey for (Date)

_____

_____

_____

_____

_____

_____

_____

_____

_____

_____

_____

_____

_____

_____

_____

_____

64. Something to Think About

Philippians 4:8 (KJV) says, "Finally, brethren, whatsoever things are true, whatsoever things *are* honest, whatsoever things *are* just, whatsoever things *are* pure, whatsoever things *are* lovely, whatsoever things *are* of good report; if *there be* any virtue, and if *there be* any praise, think on these things" (emphasis added).

One of the easiest things to do is ... think. You might not be able to think of something specific sometimes, but you can always think of something. On the other hand, it is next to impossible to not think or even to not think about something in particular. Even if you say, "I'm just not going to think about that anymore." Then you think about it by default!

So what is the answer to the whole thinking thing? You should always have something good to think about. That is where our scripture comes in. The following are some things to think about:
things that are true,
things that *are* honest,
things that *are* just,
things that *are* pure,
things that *are* lovely,
things that *are* of good report,
things that contain any virtue, and
things that contain any praise.
Think on these things.

Your mind is going to be busy thinking, so choose to only occupy it with these kinds of thoughts. That will turn your day right around. (At night you may sometimes lie down to sleep only to find that your mind is in the mood to think.) Bring every thought under the obedience of Christ. If it's not from the Lord, then it's not true, so don't think about it. If it's not a good report, don't think about it.

That's something to think about!

A Journal of My Journey for (Date)

_____

_____

_____

_____

_____

_____

_____

_____

_____

_____

_____

_____

_____

_____

_____

65. But Lord, What About That Person?

John 21:15–22 (KJV) says,

So when they had dined, Jesus saith to Simon Peter, Simon, *son* of Jonas, lovest thou me more than these? He saith unto him, Yea, Lord; thou knowest that I love thee. He saith unto him, Feed my lambs. He saith to him again the second time, Simon, *son* of Jonas, lovest thou me? He saith unto him, Yea, Lord; thou knowest that I love thee. He saith unto him, Feed my sheep. He saith unto him the third time, Simon, *son* of Jonas, lovest thou me? Peter was grieved because he said unto him the third time, Lovest thou me? And he said unto him, Lord, thou knowest all things; thou knowest that I love thee. Jesus saith unto him, Feed my sheep. Verily, verily, I say unto thee, When thou wast young, thou girdedst thyself, and walkedst whither thou wouldest: but when thou shalt be old, thou shalt stretch forth thy hands, and another shall gird thee, and carry *thee* whither thou wouldest not. This spake he, signifying by what death he should glorify God. And when he had spoken this, he saith unto him, Follow me. Then Peter, turning about, seeth the disciple whom Jesus loved following; which also leaned on his breast at supper, and said, Lord, which is he that betrayeth thee? Peter seeing him saith to Jesus, Lord, and what *shall* this man *do?* Jesus saith unto him, If I will that he tarry till I come, what *is that* to thee? follow thou me. (emphasis added)

Peter was going through a phase in his relationship with the Lord. He had seen all of the miracles and heard all of the teachings, but then when crunch time came, he denied even knowing Jesus—three times in one night!

Praise God for His forgiveness and patience. After Jesus was crucified, buried, and rose from the dead, Peter found himself at a loss as to what to do next. He was still carrying around the guilt of his denial. So as a fisherman by trade, he went fishing.

The next morning he had a close encounter with God. Jesus made breakfast for him and the others, and then He had a conversation with Peter. There is much we could say about that conversation, but let's look toward the end. Instead of focusing on what Jesus was telling him to do, Peter was busy looking around, and when Jesus gave Peter this simple command to sum it all up, Peter wasn't ready with a commitment to follow Jesus. Why? Because his eyes were not on Jesus. They were on John.

How sad it would be if Jesus were speaking to you and commissioning you to do His will and all He heard in reply was, "But Lord, what about this person or that person?" Jesus' reply is still the same today. "What is that to you? You follow Me."

"Heavenly Father, help me keep my eyes on Jesus and not look to the right or to the left and not compare my walk with You with anyone else's. Help me be content so that I can be a good steward of the calling You have entrusted to me, which is unique and special and has my name on it. Thank You for giving me a second chance. In Jesus' name. Amen."

A Journal of My Journey for (Date)

_____

_____

_____

_____

_____

_____

_____

_____

_____

_____

_____

_____

_____

_____

_____

66. How Big Is God's Love?

Ephesians 3:17–21 (KJV) says,
That Christ may dwell in your hearts by faith; that ye, being rooted and grounded in love, May be able to comprehend with all saints what *is* the breadth, and length, and depth, and height; And to know the love of Christ, which passeth knowledge, that ye might be filled with all the fulness of God. Now unto him that is able to do exceeding abundantly above all that we ask or think, according to the power that worketh in us, Unto him *be* glory in the church by Christ Jesus throughout all ages, world without end. Amen. (emphasis added)

When you think about the whole concept of love, it is natural to think of it in human terms—the limitations and conditions that come with being human. But God's love for you cannot be measured in human terms. Paul's prayer for the believers (saints) at Ephesus is for "the whole family in heaven and earth" (verse 15). By the power of the Spirit of God, you can comprehend and know that which is beyond human comprehension. Your faith and trust in Christ is rooted and grounded in His love for you.

The amazing thing about the width, length, depth, and height of God's love for you is that no matter how big our past failures are, His love is bigger! Maybe you sometimes feel like God could not love you because of one thing or another or maybe because of a multitude or reasons that you cannot forget. God's love is still bigger.

The one who knows you best loves you most. (After all, God knew all of your days before your substance was even formed in your mother's womb.) His love reaches to the heavens.

To Him be glory forever and ever. Amen.

A Journal of My Journey for (Date)

_____

_____

_____

_____

_____

_____

_____

_____

_____

_____

_____

_____

_____

_____

_____

_____

67. If the Lord Wills

James 4:13–15 (KJV) says, "Go to now, ye that say, To day or to morrow we will go into such a city, and continue there a year, and buy and sell, and get gain: Whereas ye know not what *shall be* on the morrow. For what *is* your life? It is even a vapour, that appeareth for a little time, and then vanisheth away. For that ye *ought* to say, If the Lord will, we shall live, and do this, or that" (emphasis added).

What an important reminder from James. It is so easy to get caught up in time and overlook eternity! We are on this earth for a little time, and then this physical existence vanishes away like vapor. So what then? Do I just stop living and do nothing? Nope. That is not what the Lord is saying here.

The key is not to live life apart from the Lord. Just as God is in all of His creation, so He wants to be a part of everything in your life. Maybe you need to take a step back and ask, "Lord, is it Your will for me to go here or there and do this or that?" You don't want to walk down the road and say, "Hey, Lord, uh … where are You? Can't you keep up? What's that about Your will? I just thought You would be okay with my plans."

You do not know what will happen tomorrow, but God holds all of your tomorrows in His hands. Start every step of your journey through life by saying, "If the Lord wills it," and you must mean it!

A Journal of My Journey for (Date)

_____

_____

_____

_____

_____

_____

_____

_____

_____

_____

_____

_____

_____

_____

_____

_____

68. The Working of the Word

Psalm 19:7–8 (KJV) says, "The law of the LORD *is* perfect, converting the soul: the testimony of the LORD *is* sure, making wise the simple. The statutes of the LORD *are* right, rejoicing the heart: the commandment of the LORD *is* pure, enlightening the eyes" (emphasis added).

It is amazing what God's Word can do when you give it a good place to grow. Here are four examples.

Since the Lord is perfect, so is His Law. If you try to live up to God's standard as a way of getting into heaven, you will fall short. Everyone falls short of the glory of God. Rather the Law is a tutor to lead you to Christ, your Redeemer, the one who took your place and became the perfect sacrificial Lamb. The Law teaches you that you must be converted or, as Jesus put it, "you must be born again."

Through God's Word and through Jesus (the living Word), you receive the wisdom of God. In fact, Jesus has become wisdom from God. In God's economy, it's not so much what you know as it is who you know that gives you wisdom.

By having the clear boundaries set out by the Word of God in your life and choosing to live within those boundaries, you are free in a way that allows your heart to literally rejoice. It is such a burden to try to live by your own definition of right and wrong because then you are taking the place of God, and those shoes are too big for anyone to fill!

Through God's commandments, you see the pure love of your heavenly Father, and all of a sudden, you can see that He is not trying to punish you or keep you from having fun. You realize that everything the Lord commands is for your benefit. What an eye-opener!

"Heavenly Father, I thank You for Your Word, which brought me salvation and daily gives me wisdom. Your Word is a source of joy in my heart, and through Your Word, my eyes are opened. Help me to continually have ears to hear and a heart that is ready to receive it in Jesus' name. Amen

A Journal of My Journey for (Date)

_____

_____

_____

_____

_____

_____

_____

_____

_____

_____

_____

_____

_____

_____

_____

69. Jesus, Friend of Sinners

Matthew 9:9–13 (KJV) says,
And as Jesus passed forth from thence, he saw a man, named Matthew, sitting at the receipt of custom: and he saith unto him, Follow me. And he arose, and followed him. And it came to pass, as Jesus sat at meat in the house, behold, many publicans and sinners came and sat down with him and his disciples. And when the Pharisees saw *it,* they said unto his disciples, Why eateth your Master with publicans and sinners? But when Jesus heard *that,* he said unto them, They that be whole need not a physician, but they that are sick. But go ye and learn what *that* meaneth, I will have mercy, and not sacrifice: for I am not come to call the righteous, but sinners to repentance. (emphasis added)

John 15:13–15 (KJV) says, "Greater love hath no man than this, that a man lay down his life for his friends. Ye are my friends, if ye do whatsoever I command you. Henceforth I call you not servants; for the servant knoweth not what his lord doeth: but I have called you friends; for all things that I have heard of my Father I have made known unto you."

Jesus is a friend of sinners, so we can become friends of His! It's easy to see where the Pharisees were getting their righteous indignation from. Some of the most despised people of the day were tax collectors. One day Jesus shows up at the tax office and becomes a friend to Matthew, a tax collector. Because of that encounter, Matthew meets Jesus, follows Him, and becomes His friend.

But wait! Matthew is a … sinner! Yep, that's true, but the Pharisees weren't exactly saints. (They were more like sons of snakes, according to Jesus.) Even when we were still sinners, Christ died for us. Oh, what a wonderful salvation!

But back to our true story. So Jesus goes over for a meal with his new follower (Matthew the sinner), and guess who Matthew has over for dinner. A bunch of sinners! That certainly didn't sit well with the Pharisees, but Jesus was about to teach the teachers a lesson. People who are well don't need a physician. Jesus came to call sinners to repentance, and once a sinner comes to repentance and follows Jesus, they become a friend of Jesus.

These words, which were penned by Joseph M. Scriven in 1855, come from the song, "What a Friend We Have in Jesus."
Can we find a friend so faithful,

Who will all our sorrows share?
Jesus knows our every weakness;
Take it to the Lord in prayer.

Thank the Lord for His mercy. He is a friend to us sinners, and we can become a friend of His as saints!

A Journal of My Journey for (Date)

_____

_____

_____

_____

_____

_____

_____

_____

_____

_____

_____

_____

_____

_____

70. Noah's Greatest Gift

Genesis 6:5–8 (KJV) says,

And God saw that the wickedness of man *was* great in the earth, and *that* every imagination of the thoughts of his heart *was* only evil continually. And it repented the LORD that he had made man on the earth, and it grieved him at his heart. And the LORD said, I will destroy man whom I have created from the face of the earth; both man, and beast, and the creeping thing, and the fowls of the air; for it repenteth me that I have made them. But Noah found grace in the eyes of the LORD. (emphasis added)

When you think about Noah, what comes to mind? Probably something to do with a really big boat, right? Oh, and lots of rain! Maybe you picture pairs of all kinds of animals coming to him in the ark. Maybe you think that Noah was a really gifted carpenter. Maybe you think he had a way with animals. Without a doubt, Noah was blessed by the Lord in these and probably other areas of his life, but none of these is his greatest gift.

Noah lived in a dark time. The wickedness of humankind had reached such a level that God was grieved in His heart, sorry that He had ever created humankind in the first place. That's about as bad as it gets. It may seem like people are inventing new ways to do evil, but there is nothing new under the sun. It's been done before and probably during Noah's time.

With so much evil all around, you might think it would be impossible for a person to serve God faithfully and raise his or her children to do the same, but you must remember that no matter how bad the world gets, God is always the same. He never changes, and He is able to do exceedingly abundantly above anything that we could ever even think to ask of Him.

What was Noah's greatest gift? The grace of God. You could accomplish great feats as Noah did and be busy every day doing what God wants, but without God's grace, everything else would amount to nothing. It is the grace of God that gets you an audience with the King of Kings, and it is the grace of God that gets you adoption papers to become His child.

"Father, I thank You for Your favor toward me. I thank You that You have loved me and adopted me into Your family and that You have made me a joint heir with Jesus Christ. I am blessed because You have poured Your favor on me. In Jesus' name. Amen."

A Journal of My Journey for (Date)

_____

_____

_____

_____

_____

_____

_____

_____

_____

_____

_____

_____

_____

_____

_____

71. Who Can This Be?

Luke 8:22–25 (KJV) says,
Now it came to pass on a certain day, that he went into a ship with his disciples: and he said unto them, "Let us go over unto the other side of the lake." And they launched forth. But as they sailed he fell asleep: and there came down a storm of wind on the lake; and they were filled *with water,* and were in jeopardy. And they came to him, and awoke him, saying, Master, master, we perish. Then he arose, and rebuked the wind and the raging of the water: and they ceased, and there was a calm. And he said unto them, "Where is your faith?" And they being afraid wondered, saying one to another, What manner of man is this! for he commandeth even the winds and water, and they obey him. (emphasis added)

If you were to just come upon this story without knowing the people involved, you could really miss out on a couple of important points. For instance, Jesus' disciples were fishermen by trade, so being on a boat on the lake was not something new to them. They were professionals at handling a boat. So too, without knowing Jesus, you would not realize that He is "not of this world," although by the end of the story you might begin to have your suspicions.

First, let's consider the lesson here for the disciples (and for us as well). This wasn't a lesson on fishing or how to handle a sailboat in windy weather. No, this was a lesson in faith. The Lord took them to a place where they would be most confident in their own ability. Before they met Jesus, they would probably be more comfortable and at home out on the lake with the fish than on the shore with people! Anyway, the Lord turned that situation into one that was way beyond their control. Where is Jesus during this event? He's asleep! Did they learn their lesson? Not so much. That's a bummer. Maybe we will learn something from this though.

Next, what about Jesus? He is not a fisherman by trade, and yet He could make it across the lake in His sleep! Who can this be? Jesus came into this world (which was made through Him) and lived in this world as a man. He did it perfectly. But He also brought power and authority into this world— power and authority that was not of this world. He can rebuke the weather, and it obeys Him!

"Where is your faith?" Jesus asks. And that is what He is asking you today. Do you trust Jesus with everything in your life? What about those things that you are confident in and can handle all by yourself? Have you trusted Jesus with those areas? It is a blessing when we are reminded that our Lord is not of this world. He is not limited to the laws of nature because He is above nature and all created things! There is nothing too difficult for the Lord.

Who can this be? He is Jesus the Messiah, the Word, God the Son, the great I Am, the first and the last, the Alpha and the Omega, the beginning and the end, the everlasting God, the Lord, your healer, the Prince of Peace.

Who can this be? He's the Master of the wind and waves of your life. You need only believe!

A Journal of My Journey for (Date)

72. Life Only Moves in One Direction

Jeremiah 29:11 (KJV) says, "For I know the thoughts that I think toward you, saith the LORD, thoughts of peace, and not of evil, to give you an expected end."

Everything that God has planned for you is ahead, not behind. If you spend your time in the past, then you are not living life. Life is always moving forward. Your life is ahead of you. You can save money, or you can spend it. But you can't really put time in a bottle, now can you?

Time has a way of slipping away from the present into the past.

Hope is ahead of you. The Lord is seeing to that. So what is your part in all of this? Make the most of every moment. Don't try to live in the past. That works about as well as trying to eat yesterday's manna. Go through each day remembering the importance and preciousness of the gift of life and live it to the fullest.

Ready or not, life moves on, so don't let it move on without you! Press onward with the Lord, and if you fall down, get up and run toward your calling. The God of your salvation is the God of your future. You can put your trust and confidence in Him.

Life is moving. Don't get left behind!

A Journal of My Journey for (Date)

_____

_____

_____

_____

_____

_____

_____

_____

_____

_____

_____

_____

_____

_____

_____

_____

73. Consider the Work of God's Fingers

Psalm 8:1–6 (KJV) says,
To the chief Musician upon Gittith, A Psalm of David. O LORD our Lord, how excellent *is* thy name in all the earth! who hast set thy glory above the heavens. Out of the mouth of babes and sucklings hast thou ordained strength because of thine enemies, that thou mightest still the enemy and the avenger. When I consider thy heavens, the work of thy fingers, the moon and the stars, which thou hast ordained; What is man, that thou art mindful of him? and the son of man, that thou visitest him? For thou hast made him a little lower than the angels, and hast crowned him with glory and honour. Thou madest him to have dominion over the works of thy hands; thou hast put all *things* under his feet. (emphasis added)

Sometimes things in this life can be challenging, even overwhelming at times. God has set His glory above the heavens. Looking up helps you get your perspective back. It gives you just a glimpse of God's glory.

So how does looking up help exactly? When you see the expanse of the heavens and the moon and stars, it helps you to see that since this world is merely the work of God's fingers, He can definitely come through for you.

The other thing it will do is help you put your life in perspective. If God is so awesome and He creates a masterpiece like the heavens with His fingers, what is humankind in comparison to the God of all creation? But by His mercy and grace, He has crowned you with glory and honor and given you dominion over all of the work of His hands. Through Jesus Christ, He has given you authority. All things are under your feet!

The next time you are feeling down, look up! Consider the work of His fingers. If you are feeling down, you are probably looking down or around, but as soon as you begin to look up, the Lord will lift you up.

Don't get your thoughts and emotions all clogged up with the things of this world. Consider the work of God's fingers.

A Journal of My Journey for (Date)

_____

_____

_____

_____

_____

_____

_____

_____

_____

_____

_____

_____

_____

_____

_____

_____

74. The Name above All Names

Ephesians 1:15–23 (KJV) says,
Wherefore I also, after I heard of your faith in the Lord Jesus, and love unto all the saints, Cease not to give thanks for you, making mention of you in my prayers; That the God of our Lord Jesus Christ, the Father of glory, may give unto you the spirit of wisdom and revelation in the knowledge of him: The eyes of your understanding being enlightened; that ye may know what is the hope of his calling, and what the riches of the glory of his inheritance in the saints, And what *is* the exceeding greatness of his power to us-ward who believe, according to the working of his mighty power, Which he wrought in Christ, when he raised him from the dead, and set *him* at his own right hand in the heavenly *places*, Far above all principality, and power, and might, and dominion, and every name that is named, not only in this world, but also in that which is to come: And hath put all *things* under his feet, and gave him *to be* the head over all *things* to the church, Which is his body, the fulness of him that filleth all in all. (emphasis added)

When you see how Paul was praying for the Ephesian Christians, you realize that everything you need in this life is in Jesus.

His name is above all names. Jesus Christ is above every principality. That covers the every chief in rank. He is above every power. He is above the rulers of government. He is above everyone and everything else! He is above everything in this age and also in the times to come.

That covers time and eternity.
In other words, Jesus has a name above all names. Period.
How far above? Far above. Where are all of His enemies (and your enemies)? Under His feet (and under your feet).

But how does that help you? As long as you are a part of the church, then this Jesus is the Father's gift to you. He gave Him to the church! The church is the body of Christ, and Jesus is the head.

So to sum it up, whatever you face in this life is under the feet of Jesus. It doesn't matter how big or bad or superhuman it is. Jesus is bigger.

Trust in the Lord. Rest in Him. And go forth in victory with every enemy under your feet in Jesus' name, the name above all names.

A Journal of My Journey for (Date)

_____

_____

_____

_____

_____

_____

_____

_____

_____

_____

_____

_____

_____

_____

_____

75. A Pep Talk for the Soul

Psalm 103:1–5 (KJV) says, "Bless the LORD, O my soul: and all that is within me, *bless* his holy name. Bless the LORD, O my soul, and forget not all his benefits: Who forgiveth all thine iniquities; who healeth all thy diseases; Who redeemeth thy life from destruction; who crowneth thee with lovingkindness and tender mercies; Who satisfieth thy mouth with good *things; so that* thy youth is renewed like the eagle's" (emphasis added).

This is a psalm of David, the one who as a lad stood before the giant Goliath when all of the armies of Israel (including his older brothers) were hiding in fear. That would certainly have to qualify as one of the highlights in his life. Surely, the slideshow at his wedding would have included pictures of him holding up the head of the giant after that victory. Wait. They didn't have slideshows back then. Anyway, that would have been a day he never would have forgotten.

You have had those days yourself—mountaintop experiences of one type or another. During those times it is easy to bless the Lord. But consider some other days in David's life. After he slew the giant, he found that he was the object of the mad king's jealousy, envy, and even hatred. The king would use David for target practice! But that's not the end of David's bad days. As if the treachery of the king, whom David served loyally, wasn't bad enough, he would one day face betrayal by some of his men and ... even his own son.

These are just a few of the many things that David faced during his life. So what was his secret to being a "man after God's own heart?" Here is one clue from our scripture. Sometimes you have to give your soul a pep talk. It may go something like this: "Soul, now you just get up out of that pity party and bless the Lord. Bless His holy name.

Remember, God has never done you anything but good. He forgave you. He redeemed you. He's your healer. He covers you with loving-kindness and mercy. He gives you good things, and He renews you."

You can have that talk with your soul. Remind yourself of God's goodness and bless His name. What if you don't feel like blessing the Lord? Bless Him anyway because He is worthy, and then you will see things begin to change in you. You can't always be holding up a giant's head in victory, but you can bless the Lord every day. Even if it takes a pep talk for your soul!

A Journal of My Journey for (Date)

76. Lift Up the Lord

Exodus 15:1–6 (KJV) says,

Then sang Moses and the children of Israel this song unto the LORD, and spake, saying, I will sing unto the LORD, for he hath triumphed gloriously: the horse and his rider hath he thrown into the sea. The LORD *is* my strength and song, and he is become my salvation: he *is* my God, and I will prepare him an habitation; my father's God, and I will exalt him. The LORD *is* a man of war: the LORD *is* his name. Pharaoh's chariots and his host hath he cast into the sea: his chosen captains also are drowned in the Red sea. The depths have covered them: they sank into the bottom as a stone. Thy right hand, O LORD, is become glorious in power: thy right hand, O LORD, hath dashed in pieces the enemy. (emphasis added)

Ah, the thrill of victory! It is fitting to sing such a song of praise to God when He has worked the greatest of all miracles—your deliverance from Egypt. Moses stood before Pharaoh and gave him ultimatum after ultimatum. God knew how it would unfold, and He told Moses ahead of time how it was going to go. Finally, the time came—Passover. Every house whose doorposts and lintels were covered with the blood of the lamb was spared, but the rest were not protected. It was enough to bring even the mighty Pharaoh into alignment with God's plan—at least for a little while. He should have just let them go and moved on, but no, he would have to lose his army and his weapons of war in the Red Sea before it sunk in that God was bigger!

So here God's people are singing and shouting the victory until a few verses later. Consider what's happening in the wilderness.

Exodus 15:22–27 (KJV) says,

So Moses brought Israel from the Red sea, and they went out into the wilderness of Shur; and they went three days in the wilderness, and found no water. And when they came to Marah, they could not drink of the waters of Marah, for they *were* bitter: therefore the name of it was called Marah. And the people murmured against Moses, saying, What shall we drink? And he cried unto the LORD; and the LORD showed him a tree, *which* when he had cast into the waters, the waters were made sweet: there he made for them a statute and an ordinance, and there he proved them, And said, If thou wilt diligently hearken to the voice of the LORD thy God, and wilt do that which is right in his sight, and wilt give ear to his commandments, and keep all his statutes, I will put none of these diseases upon thee, which I have brought upon the Egyptians: for I *am* the LORD that healeth thee. And they came to Elim, where *were* twelve wells of water, and threescore and ten palm trees: and they encamped there by the waters. (emphasis added)

It only took them three days to forget their song of victory and take up that all familiar tune of "woe is me." Praise God for His patience and mercy!

"Heavenly Father, help me not to be a fair-weather Christian, only praising You when everything is going my way. Give me the strength and faith to praise You before I cross over the Red Sea. Give me the fortitude to praise You even when I can't see where the next drink of water is coming from. Lord, I want to lift You up every day no matter what happens. In Jesus' name. Amen."

A Journal of My Journey for (Date)

77. Special People

First Peter 2:9–10 (KJV) says, "But ye *are* a chosen generation, a royal priesthood, an holy nation, a peculiar people; that ye should show forth the praises of him who hath called you out of darkness into his marvellous light: Which in time past *were* not a people, but *are* now the people of God: which had not obtained mercy, but now have obtained mercy" (emphasis added).

Everyone likes to feel special. Many people go to great lengths to try to feel special. Maybe you have some days when you feel special and other days where you don't. (God's Word is truth, so we can know without a doubt what the truth is.) And the truth is that you are special every day. You are a unique creation of God, and what He created you to be is very good.

What is the key to experiencing that *specialness* in your life every day? Let's have a look at our scripture. We see right off that it is all about God and His love and mercy toward us. Because of who He is, you are chosen, royalty, holy, God's own, one called out of darkness into His light, and blessed with the mercy of God.

Put all of that together, and what does that make you? Special!

Now for those who have not yet been adopted into God's family through faith in the Lord Jesus Christ, this can be your day. Receive the mercy of God today. By faith, accept Jesus Christ as your Lord and Savior, and you will also be ... special. You can't earn it or be good enough for it, but you can accept the free gift of salvation through faith.

Once you have become a part of the people of God, you are a part of God's own special people!

A Journal of My Journey for (Date)

_____

_____

_____

_____

_____

_____

_____

_____

_____

_____

_____

_____

_____

_____

_____

78. Glory in the Lord

First Corinthians 1:26–31 (KJV) says,

For ye see your calling, brethren, how that not many wise men after the flesh, not many mighty, not many noble, *are called:* But God hath chosen the foolish things of the world to confound the wise; and God hath chosen the weak things of the world to confound the things which are mighty; And base things of the world, and things which are despised, hath God chosen, *yea,* and things which are not, to bring to nought things that are: That no flesh should glory in his presence. But of him are ye in Christ Jesus, who of God is made unto us wisdom, and righteousness, and sanctification, and redemption: That, according as it is written, He that glorieth, let him glory in the Lord. (emphasis added)

It is a relief to know that our standing with God is not based on who or what we are. It's not based on our wisdom or knowledge. It's not based on our righteousness. It's really quite the opposite. God takes broken vessels and makes them into beautiful works of His hands when they are willing to yield to His touch.

Look at the choices the Lord has made—the foolish things, the weak things, the despised things. But why doesn't He seek after the most gifted, the most talented, the wisest, the strongest? Doesn't it seem like there are many better choices than the ones He has chosen? So why these choices? He chose this way so that no flesh should glory in His presence.

Your life is to be a reflection of the glory of God. God blesses you with gifts and talents—abilities that are from His hand. But it is not for the sake of bringing glory to you but rather to point people to Jesus. He has become for you wisdom, righteousness, sanctification, and redemption. All glory goes to the Father through our Lord Jesus Christ.

All that you have and all that you are is because of the goodness of God. Don't glory in those things or those abilities or even the accomplishments of this life. Glory in the Lord!

A Journal of My Journey for (Date)

_____

_____

_____

_____

_____

_____

_____

_____

_____

_____

_____

_____

_____

_____

_____

_____

79. Confident in Christ

Philippians 1:3–6 (KJV) says, "I thank my God upon every remembrance of you, Always in every prayer of mine for you all making request with joy, For your fellowship in the gospel from the first day until now; Being confident of this very thing, that he which hath begun a good work in you will perform *it* until the day of Jesus Christ" (emphasis added).

There are plenty of things not to be sure of in this world. That is why it is vital to put your confidence in that which is "not of this world." Jesus told Pilate that His kingdom is not of this world. It is not from here.

That is an important distinction. The kingdom of heaven is at hand. It has come near you. It is here, but it is not *from* here. There is nothing of this world for you to put your confidence in, but there is someone from another world on whom you can rely completely.

Jesus Christ is your solid Rock. The Father has begun the good work in you, and He will complete it! The Lord will never leave you or forsake you. Jesus Christ and His Word are always the same. They never change.

If you have received Jesus Christ as your Lord and Savior, you can be confident that your past is forgiven and forgotten. You can be confident that He is aware of where you are right now and He is with you. You can be confident that He will complete the work He started in you right up until the moment He takes you home. Put your future in His hands and rest in Him.

A Journal of My Journey for (Date)

_____

_____

_____

_____

_____

_____

_____

_____

_____

_____

_____

_____

_____

_____

80. Serve the Lord with Gladness

Psalm 100 (KJV) says, "Make a joyful noise unto the LORD, all ye lands. Serve the LORD with gladness: come before his presence with singing. Know ye that the LORD he *is* God: *it is* he *that* hath made us, and not we ourselves; *we are* his people, and the sheep of his pasture. Enter into his gates with thanksgiving, *and* into his courts with praise: be thankful unto him, *and* bless his name. For the LORD *is* good; his mercy *is* everlasting; and his truth *endureth* to all generations" (emphasis added).

Wouldn't it be great to go through life each day with joy and gladness, thanksgiving and praise, and singing and blessing the Lord and being thankful to Him? So if that would be such a great way to live, why is it so difficult to attain? A lot of it has to do with your approach to life in general.

First, you must acknowledge the Lord as the Lord. Give a joyful shout to the Lord. God's justification for giving us commands, and our reason to obey those commands really boils down to this one truth, as He says, "for I am the Lord your God." That's it. God is God, and we are not. Trying to be God can be very tiring and frustrating and a bummer in general, so just let I Am be I Am, and you be you.

Next, you must acknowledge that you are His servant. Serve the Lord with gladness. You don't want to go through life serving the Lord just because you have to. We should not serve the Lord begrudgingly but gladly. Verse 3 helps with that. It is He who has made us. We are His people, His sheep, and we live in His pasture.

And finally, what do we have to be so happy and joyous about? The three maxims are enough to last a lifetime—God is good, His mercy knows no end, and His truth never changes. When you face each day with these truths in mind, it becomes natural to rejoice in the Lord and to bless His name. Serve the Lord with gladness. There's every reason to and no reason not to!

A Journal of My Journey for (Date)

_____

_____

_____

_____

_____

_____

_____

_____

_____

_____

_____

_____

_____

_____

_____

81. God Is Greater

First John 4:1–4 (KJV) says,

Beloved, believe not every spirit, but try the spirits whether they are of God: because many false prophets are gone out into the world. Hereby know ye the Spirit of God: Every spirit that confesseth that Jesus Christ is come in the flesh is of God: And every spirit that confesseth not that Jesus Christ is come in the flesh is not of God: and this is that *spirit* of antichrist, whereof ye have heard that it should come; and even now already is it in the world. Ye are of God, little children, and have overcome them: because greater is he that is in you, than he that is in the world. (emphasis added)

This world is full of imposters and pretenders and usurpers. But in the midst of them all, there is the one true God who is greater—bigger than all of them put together. That is why you can overcome all of the evil in this world. The one who is in you is greater than he who is in the world.

Why is this test for spirits so important? Because it goes to the heart of the gospel of Christ. Jesus Christ came to the earth in the flesh as a man so that He could take the sin of all the world upon Himself as a perfect sacrifice for our sins. Anyone who comes bringing any other gospel is not of God. They have the spirit of the antichrist.

If someone comes proclaiming that Jesus was just a good teacher and the Bible is just another old book with some suggestions and metaphors in it and that we need a new definition of things for a new millennium, your antichrist alarm should sound at full blast! You either have to believe the Bible in its entirety or not believe it at all. You have to take Jesus as everything He said He was and all the Bible says He is or not at all.

But it seems like we are outnumbered greatly in this world. Everywhere you look, there are people who try to convince you there is no God, and they live their lives accordingly. The entertainment industry, academia, as well as most forms of media both online and offline seem to be filled with those who are pushing this agenda. So what can you do against such odds? Simply remember this: When you are on the Lord's side, you are always on the winning team. God is greater!

A Journal of My Journey for (Date)

_____

_____

_____

_____

_____

_____

_____

_____

_____

_____

_____

_____

_____

_____

_____

82. Look at the Fields

John 4:31–38 (KJV) says,
In the mean while his disciples prayed him, saying, Master, eat. But he said unto them, "I have meat to eat that ye know not of." Therefore said the disciples one to another, Hath any man brought him *ought* to eat? Jesus saith unto them, "My meat is to do the will of him that sent me, and to finish his work. Say not ye, There are yet four months, and *then* cometh harvest? behold, I say unto you, Lift up your eyes, and look on the fields; for they are white already to harvest. And he that reapeth receiveth wages, and gathereth fruit unto life eternal: that both he that soweth and he that reapeth may rejoice together. And herein is that saying true, One soweth, and another reapeth. I sent you to reap that whereon ye bestowed no labour: other men laboured, and ye are entered into their labours." (emphasis added)

Today, just as in Jesus' time on the earth, there are people all around who need the Lord. "Look at the fields," He says. Then He goes on to talk about sowing and reaping the fruit for eternal life. Jesus is just using the natural world to teach us a spiritual lesson and to show us truths that cannot be seen with the eye.

You probably already picked up on Jesus' metaphor, but maybe you sometimes feel like your life is already too full of things to add sowing, reaping, and harvesting to the list. You know there are people all around who need Jesus, but surely He has someone else in mind who can get the job done, right?

Maybe you think, *God can't use me because I have a past.* The good news is that if you have made Jesus your Lord and Savior, Jesus took your past upon Himself on that cross. The old you was buried with Christ, and you are a new you! Everyone in God's kingdom had a past that only the blood of the perfect Lamb of God could cover!

Okay then. What about this excuse? "I am busy every waking moment of my life taking care of something." Maybe you have small children or aging parents who seem to consume all of your time, or your job could take seemingly all of your time. Whatever it is, more than likely it involves people—little people, big people, young or old people, people you are related to or people you hardly know. However, that may be one of the very *fields* Jesus is telling you to look at.

Whatever you do to Jesus' brethren, you do unto Him. You may find plenty of opportunities for sowing, reaping, and harvesting all around you in your daily life. Just look at the fields!

A Journal of My Journey for (Date)

83. A Very Present Help

Psalm 46:1–3 (KJV) says, "To the chief Musician for the sons of Korah, A Song upon Alamoth. God *is* our refuge and strength, a very present help in trouble. Therefore will not we fear, though the earth be removed, and though the mountains be carried into the midst of the sea; *Though* the waters thereof roar *and* be troubled, *though* the mountains shake with the swelling thereof. Selah" (emphasis added).

Jesus said that there would be trouble in this world. Maybe even your mamma said there'd be days like this. At any rate, there will be some times in your life when you need help. Peter faced one of those moments when he was walking on water. Actually, his day was going pretty swell at first. After all, it's not every day that Jesus invites you to go for a walk with Him—on water! Anyway, speaking of swell, Peter began to notice the wind and the waves. Those swells were pretty high. And then his troubles began. Peter began to sink. But he had time and the presence of mind to utter these three words: "Lord, save me."

Just like Peter, there are times when a God would not be able to help when you really need Him. But you need not fear. God is a very present help in times of trouble. He is your refuge from the storm, and He is your strength when you are weak. When you look at the examples the psalmist provides, you see they are extreme circumstances— mountains thrown into the sea, the sea so troubled and swelled that the mountains shake. The point is that no matter how bad things get all around you, there is nothing to fear, for your God is with you through the fire, through the flood, and through all of the trouble you face in this world.

God is a very present help!

A Journal of My Journey for (Date)

_____

_____

_____

_____

_____

_____

_____

_____

_____

_____

_____

_____

_____

_____

_____

84. Holy Ground

Exodus 3:1–8 (KJV) says,

Now Moses kept the flock of Jethro his father in law, the priest of Midian: and he led the flock to the backside of the desert, and came to the mountain of God, *even* to Horeb. And the angel of the LORD appeared unto him in a flame of fire out of the midst of a bush: and he looked, and, behold, the bush burned with fire, and the bush *was* not consumed. And Moses said, I will now turn aside, and see this great sight, why the bush is not burnt. And when the LORD saw that he turned aside to see, God called unto him out of the midst of the bush, and said, Moses, Moses. And he said, Here *am* I. And he said, Draw not nigh hither: put off thy shoes from off thy feet, for the place whereon thou standest *is* holy ground. Moreover he said, I *am* the God of thy father, the God of Abraham, the God of Isaac, and the God of Jacob. And Moses hid his face; for he was afraid to look upon God. And the LORD said, I have surely seen the affliction of my people which *are* in Egypt, and have heard their cry by reason of their taskmasters; for I know their sorrows; And I am come down to deliver them out of the hand of the Egyptians, and to bring them up out of that land unto a good land and a large, unto a land flowing with milk and honey. (emphasis added)

Moses had been saved at birth in a little baby ark, adopted by Pharaoh's daughter, nursed and brought up by his Hebrew mother, all the while growing up as the son of Pharaoh's daughter. But he chose to be called a child of God and counted with the people of God. Where did that get him? Well, he ended up on the back side of the wilderness taking care of someone else's sheep. That does not exactly seem like the road to success. How would it sound when you come to the end of your days on this earth and hear someone say, "He had everything—wealth, power, education. The opportunities were endless, and he threw it all away to follow the God of his fathers."

When you look at Moses's life up to this point, it's rather symmetrical—years in Egypt and years in the wilderness. It would seem like that was the end of the story, but wait. God is just getting started! Moses would go on to serve God as the deliverer of His people and live many years.

You might feel stuck in Egypt as if there's no way out. Or maybe you have gotten out of Egypt only to find yourself in the wilderness with no hope of ever getting out. Just remember Moses. Remain faithful to the Lord, and you will find yourself on holy ground.

Holy ground is that place where you have an encounter with the God who created you for His divine purpose; that place where He calls you by name and commissions you for His purpose; that place where He finds you, picks you up, and tells you to run on in your race for Him!

A Journal of My Journey for (Date)

85. Childlike Faith

Matthew 21:14–16 (KJV) says,
And the blind and the lame came to him in the temple; and he healed them. And when the chief priests and scribes saw the wonderful things that he did, and the children crying in the temple, and saying, Hosanna to the son of David; they were sore displeased, And said unto him, Hearest thou what these say? And Jesus saith unto them, Yea; have ye never read, Out of the mouth of babes and sucklings thou hast perfected praise?

Matthew 18:1–4 (KJV) says,
At the same time came the disciples unto Jesus, saying, Who is the greatest in the kingdom of heaven? And Jesus called a little child unto him, and set him in the midst of them, And said, Verily I say unto you, Except ye be converted, and become as little children, ye shall not enter into the kingdom of heaven. Whosoever therefore shall humble himself as this little child, the same is greatest in the kingdom of heaven.

Have you ever wondered how God measures greatness in His kingdom? Since He is so great, you would think it would take a rather extraordinary person to achieve greatness in the kingdom of heaven, right?

It seems like the two groups that are generally the most overlooked are the ones from whom we can learn the most, namely little children and the aged. Jesus is doing wonderful things in the temple, and the children just express their praise to God without a thought to what the religious leaders are going to say about it! Jesus goes so far as to proclaim the praise of children "perfect praise." We also see that Jesus proclaimed that the measure of greatness in His kingdom is not based on a person's greatness but rather on his or her childlike humility before God.

But what about the aged? The Bible is very clear about the place of respect and honor they are due. Interestingly, we see the transition almost back to a childlike dependence when a person reaches the final season of life. Learn from the aged and from the children.

Be converted and become as a little child in your relationship with your Lord and Savior. Never be ashamed to praise Jesus openly and freely no matter who is around. This is something we see exemplified in King David, a man after God's own heart.

Also, learn the lesson of the aged and let your faith be that of a child with a dependence upon God and humility before Him.

"Heavenly Father, help me to have a childlike faith, not trusting in my own greatness but finding my place in Your kingdom through humility and dependence upon You. In Jesus' name. Amen."

A Journal of My Journey for (Date)

86. The Lord, Your Healer

Exodus 15:26 (KJV) says, "And said, If thou wilt diligently hearken to the voice of the LORD thy God, and wilt do that which is right in his sight, and wilt give ear to his commandments, and keep all his statutes, I will put none of these diseases upon thee, which I have brought upon the Egyptians: for I *am* the LORD that healeth thee" (emphasis added).

There are many ways the Lord refers to Himself throughout the Word of God, and all of them reveal something of His nature and His attributes. This is a beautiful example as we see the Lord reveal Himself to us a Jehovah Rapha, the Lord who heals.

So what does this mean for you on a day-to-day basis? First, you know that God is able to heal. He is omnipotent. Furthermore, you know that God created people to be healthy and have dominion over the rest of His creation. During the six days of creation, the Lord looked at all He created and proclaimed it to be good. When He got to day six, that day's work was "very good."

In other words, God's plan for humankind is health and wellness. It is a very good plan. What is the problem then? Sin. So just because I have sinned, I cannot be well? No, that's not it. Sin entered the world through the first man, Adam, and with sin came death. The effect of sin on all humankind is manifested through sickness among many other ways.

That brings us back to our scripture. God knows that we are just so much dust and that we all have sinned. We are all going to suffer some physical battles throughout our lives, but living the life laid out in the Word of God keeps us from suffering many things that living a life without God results in. Also, as Christians, we have the prayer of faith and the prayer of agreement. We have the laying on of hands and the anointing with oil. These were all given to us as a means of being healed in a supernatural way. Many of Jesus' miracles revolved around physical healing. Many of the miracles in the church since its birth on the day of Pentecost revolve around physical healing.

So how does the Lord want you to approach sickness and disease either in your life or in the lives of those you love? Pray and ask God for healing.

Believe it. Confess it. Proclaim it. Our God is Jehovah Rapha.

A Journal of My Journey for (Date)

87. The Right Time to Praise the Lord

Psalm 34:1 (KJV) says, "I will bless the LORD at all times: his praise *shall* continually *be* in my mouth" (emphasis added).

Well, there you have it. The right time to praise the Lord is ... all the time! That may be easier said than done. After all, when everything is going your way, it is easy, even natural, to praise the Lord. You believe in God and in His goodness, so you don't hesitate to praise the Lord during those times.

But then we come to those other times when things aren't going exactly as you had hoped or maybe even not at all as you had hoped. In fact, you may even wonder at times if the Lord even heard your prayer. Maybe you should have sent an email to heaven or a special delivery with a signature request to be sure it even got to the Lord in the first place.

No matter what is going on in your life, one sure way to make things better is to bless the Lord and to praise Him. If things are going great, then praise Him for what He is doing in your life. If things are not going so great, then praise Him for who He is, what He has done, and what He promised He will do.

All the time is the right time to praise the Lord!

A Journal of My Journey for (Date)

_____

_____

_____

_____

_____

_____

_____

_____

_____

_____

_____

_____

_____

_____

_____

_____

_____

88. Sing a New Song

Psalm 98:1–3 (KJV) says, "O sing unto the LORD a new song; for he hath done marvellous things: his right hand, and his holy arm, hath gotten him the victory. The LORD hath made known his salvation: his righteousness hath he openly showed in the sight of the heathen. He hath remembered his mercy and his truth toward the house of Israel: all the ends of the earth have seen the salvation of our God."

It is important to remember that God made times and seasons for our benefit, not His. God is the great I Am. He is eternal and forever the same. So why is it so important for us to have times and seasons? Evening and morning? The seasons of the year? Weeks and months? We can never do yesterday over, but we can get a fresh start in the morning!

The psalmist exhorts us to "sing to the Lord a new song," but why? He gives us a few things to get the song started. You could get the first verse of your new song started off with some of the many marvelous things God has done for you. Remembering (and singing about) God's faithfulness in your life helps you to trust Him today and trust Him with your tomorrows. Okay, what about a chorus or a refrain for your new song, something that you will come back to after every verse? Again, the psalmist comes through for you! That would be His salvation. Every day, that should be your refrain. "Thank You, Lord, for saving my soul."

Let's get a few more verses in here before the song ends. Actually, the song never ends. Since it is a new song, it is new every day! How about if verse two of your new song has something about His righteousness revealed through our Lord and Savior Jesus Christ, who has become for us righteousness from God? As for verse three, we can praise His mercy.

What's next? You can return to the refrain and sing about His great salvation. And then comes the fourth verse. We can sing about God's faithfulness. Wow, what a song, and to think it's new every morning!

Now it is time to bring the song to a close, so what will that look like in your new song? The salvation of our God.

What's the right way to go through each day? You should sing a new song to the Lord.

A Journal of My Journey for (Date)

_____

_____

_____

_____

_____

_____

_____

_____

_____

_____

_____

_____

_____

_____

_____

89. God Will Provide

Genesis 22:1–8 (KJV) says,

And it came to pass after these things, that God did tempt Abraham, and said unto him, Abraham: and he said, Behold, *here* I *am*. And he said, Take now thy son, thine only *son* Isaac, whom thou lovest, and get thee into the land of Moriah; and offer him there for a burnt offering upon one of the mountains which I will tell thee of. And Abraham rose up early in the morning, and saddled his ass, and took two of his young men with him, and Isaac his son, and clave the wood for the burnt offering, and rose up, and went unto the place of which God had told him. Then on the third day Abraham lifted up his eyes, and saw the place afar off. And Abraham said unto his young men, Abide ye here with the ass; and I and the lad will go yonder and worship, and come again to you. And Abraham took the wood of the burnt offering, and laid *it* upon Isaac his son; and he took the fire in his hand, and a knife; and they went both of them together. And Isaac spake unto Abraham his father, and said, My father: and he said, Here *am* I, my son. And he said, Behold the fire and the wood: but where *is* the lamb for a burnt offering? And Abraham said, My son, God will provide himself a lamb for a burnt offering: so they went both of them together. (emphasis added)

You will notice that the title of today's devotional leaves no wiggle room. It's not about what God might do or what He could do or what you wish He would do. This is about what God will do.

To fully grasp the context, we have to realize the significance of verse 2, which introduces "thine only son Isaac." The Lord promised Abraham that He would bless him with a son, and through that son Abraham's descendants would become as numerous as the stars! And here's the important part. Abraham believed God, and the Lord accounted his faith as righteousness. So we see that this was not Abraham's first test, and once again, he passes the test.

Abraham believed God again. He tells the young men with them, "We will come back to you," and to Isaac, he says, "God will provide for Himself the lamb for a burnt offering." And God did just that, and not only on that day. On another day, He provided the Lamb for the sacrifice to take our place!

What then can you take away from this example? To believe that God will provide, you must think as though He will provide. You must talk as though He will provide, and you must walk as though He will provide. And when you get to the top of the mountain of the Lord and it's time to make a sacrifice, Jehovah Jireh will always keep His Word!

God will provide.

A Journal of My Journey for (Date)

90. Say So

Psalm 107:1–9 (KJV) says,
O give thanks unto the LORD, for *he is* good: for his mercy *endureth* for ever. Let the redeemed of the LORD say *so,* whom he hath redeemed from the hand of the enemy; And gathered them out of the lands, from the east, and from the west, from the north, and from the south. They wandered in the wilderness in a solitary way; they found no city to dwell in. Hungry and thirsty, their soul fainted in them. Then they cried unto the LORD in their trouble, *and* he delivered them out of their distresses. And he led them forth by the right way, that they might go to a city of habitation. Oh that *men* would praise the LORD *for* his goodness, and *for* his wonderful works to the children of men! For he satisfieth the longing soul, and filleth the hungry soul with goodness. (emphasis added)

Which do you think would be easier—to say positive things about yourself and your life in general or to say negative things? Well, interestingly enough, it seems the answer is generally the latter.

We should speak of ourselves as God does instead of sometimes saying just the opposite. The psalmist gives us some guidance. For instance, God is good, and He made you in His image. That means you have the potential for good things!

God's mercy is His favor toward you even when you do not deserve it. That means that even when you don't feel like you are up for the Christian of the Year Award, His goodness and mercy are still following you all the days of your life!

If you are redeemed in the Lord, then say so! Don't talk about yourself according to the way you feel about yourself. Talk about yourself the way your Redeemer talks about you. Talk about His goodness toward you and the wonderful works He has done for you. Talk about how He satisfies and fills your soul with goodness!

Have you been redeemed by the blood of the Lamb of God? Well, then say so!

A Journal of My Journey for (Date)

_____

_____

_____

_____

_____

_____

_____

_____

_____

_____

_____

_____

_____

_____

_____

_____

_____

91. Spiritual Fruit

Galatians 5:22–25 (KJV) says, "But the fruit of the Spirit is love, joy, peace, longsuffering, gentleness, goodness, faith, Meekness, temperance: against such there is no law. And they that are Christ's have crucified the flesh with the affections and lusts. If we live in the Spirit, let us also walk in the Spirit."

One way to determine the contents of a container is to squeeze it and see what comes out! When you are squeezed, what comes out? You can determine the source of the contents by having a look at the list the apostle Paul gives us in our passage. Does the fruit of the Spirit comes out, or do the works of the flesh emerge?

When you allow the Spirit of God to take control of your life, you will see more and more of His inward working showing up on the outside. This list can provide some guidance in prayer so that you can yield your life to the will and purpose of God, who created you.

"Heavenly Father, I thank You that I am filled with Your Spirit, and with Your help, I will walk in love every day. I will have the joy and peace that only comes from being in Your presence. May my life be filled with the fruit of kindness and goodness. Help me to be faithful and not grow weary. Father, by the power of Your Spirit within me, let me show forth the fruit of gentleness as I walk every moment of every day in self-control. I yield my life to Your Spirit in Jesus' name. Amen."

A Journal of My Journey for (Date)

_____

_____

_____

_____

_____

_____

_____

_____

_____

_____

_____

_____

_____

_____

_____

_____

_____

_____

92. The Great Commandment

Deuteronomy 6:4–5 (KJV) says, "Hear, O Israel: The LORD our God *is* one LORD: And thou shalt love the LORD thy God with all thine heart, and with all thy soul, and with all thy might" (emphasis added).

When Jesus was asked about the greatest of all commandments, He did not hesitate. All Jews know the answer to that question, and as Christians, we do as well.

Let's break it down. First, as always, it begins by acknowledging that there is one and only one God. He is the Trinity—the Father, the Son, and the Holy Spirit—but there is only one God. Then once we identify the object of our worship, we get the details of the command. However, He must be "your God" before this works!

The great commandment says to love your God will all your heart. There is no room for any other gods on the throne of your heart. You shall have no other gods before the Lord. That sounds simple, but it may take some time at the altar in His presence to dethrone some things that may have too high of a place in your life. Let the Holy Spirit show you if there is anything there.

Next, love the Lord, your God, with all your soul. Your soul includes your mind, your will, and your emotions. When you obey this part of the command, you will find that you have more peace and joy than you have ever experienced in your life!

And finally, love the Lord your God with all your strength. Give your life over to serving the Lord and living for Him. When the Lord occupies the top spot in your life, you will find that the desire to serve Him and please Him grows. More and more you will seek His will and not your own.

"Heavenly Father, I want to obey the great commandment—to love you with all of my spirit, soul, and body—and I commit to that right now in Jesus' name. Amen."

A Journal of My Journey for (Date)

---

93. God's Math

John 12:24–26 (KJV) says, "Verily, verily, I say unto you, Except a corn of wheat fall into the ground and die, it abideth alone: but if it die, it bringeth forth much fruit. He that loveth his life shall lose it; and he that hateth his life in this world shall keep it unto life eternal. If any man serve me, let him follow me; and where I am, there shall also my servant be: if any man serve me, him will *my* Father honour" (emphasis added).

Are you good at math? It seems like math is one of those subjects that you either love or don't! When have you ever heard someone say, "Math? I can take it or leave it." No, feelings toward math are usually very well defined.

Anyway, what's math got to do with our verses for today? Let's see, one minus one usually equals zero. And if you have zero of something, that means you have nothing. I see you really are good at this math thing! God's math doesn't work like our math. In fact, in many ways it is quite the opposite. For instance, if you have a wheat seed and you keep it safe and sound, you will always have one wheat seed. But what happens if you plant it? It dies. That's where it would be natural to assume that you now have no wheat seeds.

How is this helping? Just like the wheat seed, we must be willing to give our life to the Lord, to allow our life to grow into what God created us to be. That wheat was created by God to be fruitful and multiply, to bring forth more wheat. Then we get the following equation from God's economy: One minus one equals much.

There may be things in your life that need to die and be left at the altar so that God can bring forth the fruit that He intends in your life. Change is hard. It is uncertain, and it is easier to leave things the way they are. But the Lord wants to do things in your life if you are willing to plant some seeds and let them be born again. Let God have those seeds you have been holding on to, and you will see what great things He will do!

A Journal of My Journey for (Date)

_____

_____

_____

_____

_____

_____

_____

_____

_____

_____

_____

_____

_____

_____

_____

_____

_____

94. More than Conquerors

Romans 8:35–39 (KJV) says,

Who shall separate us from the love of Christ? *shall* tribulation, or distress, or persecution, or famine, or nakedness, or peril, or sword? As it is written, For thy sake we are killed all the day long; we are accounted as sheep for the slaughter. Nay, in all these things we are more than conquerors through him that loved us. For I am persuaded, that neither death, nor life, nor angels, nor principalities, nor powers, nor things present, nor things to come, Nor height, nor depth, nor any other creature, shall be able to separate us from the love of God, which is in Christ Jesus our Lord. (emphasis added)

As a Christian in a fallen world under the sway of the wicked one, you will face at least a bit of tribulation at some time or another. The things we see in this passage seem to be the extreme examples, yet at this moment, there are Christians in parts of the world suffering extreme persecution just because they confess Jesus as Lord.

When we consider the things we go through for being Christian and give thought to those suffering severely for their faith, we may ask, "Lord, why can't you do something?" Of course, upon further reflection, we know that God indeed can do anything. Why then doesn't He do something?

To understand the answers to these and other similar questions, we have to change our perspective. We can't just see things as they are at the moment, but with eyes of faith, we must see things as they will be when it's all been said and done. This scripture and so many others tell us that we are victorious and that we live happily ever after in the end!

So what is the Lord telling us? Even in the midst of hard times, you are more than a conqueror. There is no question who the winner is.

Through Jesus Christ, you have the victory. When you pass through the fire or through the water, the Lord is always with you. And in the end, you will still have Jesus, and He will still have you.

So rejoice in the Lord, feed on His faithfulness, proclaim His goodness, and always lift up the name of Jesus. Through Him, you are more than a conqueror!

A Journal of My Journey for (Date)

_____

_____

_____

_____

_____

_____

_____

_____

_____

_____

_____

_____

_____

_____

_____

_____

95. No Condemnation

Romans 8:1–3 (KJV) says, "*There is* therefore now no condemnation to them which are in Christ Jesus, who walk not after the flesh, but after the Spirit. For the law of the Spirit of life in Christ Jesus hath made me free from the law of sin and death. For what the law could not do, in that it was weak through the flesh, God sending his own Son in the likeness of sinful flesh, and for sin, condemned sin in the flesh" (emphasis added).

Have you ever felt condemned? By others? Maybe even by yourself? Have you ever felt like God could not love you because of things you have said or done in the past? But you can never go back and change the past. You are stuck with your past. There doesn't seem to be any way to escape condemnation since we all have pasts.

The law of the Lord is perfect, but we are not. That is why the scripture says that the law is weak through the flesh. If only you could live up to every letter of God's law, you could live a perfect life, and there would be no condemnation. But alas, the flesh tempts us!

The good news is that Jesus is here for us. He came to the earth in the likeness of sinful flesh as a man. Jesus lived a perfect, sinless life on the earth and became for us a perfect sacrifice for sin. Jesus conquered sin and death.

So what do we do about our pasts, especially as the enemy (and maybe a few others) is always reminding us about them? Put it under the blood of Jesus. Receive His perfect sacrifice for your past and leave it behind so that you can press on in the Lord.

There is absolutely no condemnation to those who are in Christ Jesus. Let that be you!

A Journal of My Journey for (Date)

_____

_____

_____

_____

_____

_____

_____

_____

_____

_____

_____

_____

_____

_____

_____

_____

_____

96. The Eternal King

First Timothy 1:17 (KJV) says, "Now unto the King eternal, immortal, invisible, the only wise God, *be* honour and glory for ever and ever. Amen" (emphasis added).

When you look back through the history of nations, civilizations, and kingdoms, you see how temporary they all are in the grand scheme of things. How many kings have risen to power only to be killed by people close to them (many times even members of their families). Entire empires and civilizations have fallen. All of this stands in stark contrast to our king.

As David puts it in Psalm 24, "Who is this King of Glory? The Lord strong and mighty. The Lord mighty in battle. The Lord of Hosts." His name is Jesus. He is the King eternal. His kingdom will never come to an end. He is immortal. He defeated death, hell, and the grave. He is invisible. God is spirit, and the only way to worship Him is in spirit and truth. He alone is wise. He has all wisdom. He is wisdom from the Father for us.

This is the source of your confidence every day—that you serve this King, the King of Kings and the Lord of Lords, the Alpha and the Omega, the beginning and the end, the everlasting one.

To Jesus give all honor and glory for as long as He is King!

A Journal of My Journey for (Date)

97. The Glory of His Presence

Second Chronicles 5:7–14 (KJV) says,
And the priests brought in the ark of the covenant of the LORD unto his place, to the oracle of the house, into the most holy *place, even* under the wings of the cherubims: … *There was* nothing in the ark save the two tables which Moses put *therein* at Horeb, when the LORD made *a covenant* with the children of Israel, when they came out of Egypt. … It came even to pass, as the trumpeters and singers *were* as one, to make one sound to be heard in praising and thanking the LORD; and when they lifted up *their* voice with the trumpets and cymbals and instruments of music, and praised the LORD, *saying,* For *he is* good; for his mercy *endureth* for ever: that *then* the house was filled with a cloud, *even* the house of the LORD; So that the priests could not stand to minister by reason of the cloud: for the glory of the LORD had filled the house of God. (emphasis added)

It is wonderful to revisit this time in the history of God's relationship with humankind. David had to pass on the task of finishing the temple to his son. Now it is completed, and they are bringing in the ark of the covenant; the place where God's presence is manifested for the one who is able to enter! Indeed, God met with His people there that day.

Wouldn't it be great to experience the glory of God's presence? You can! When Jesus died on the cross, the veil in the temple that separated the people from the presence of God was torn in two from top to bottom. Jesus opened up the way for us into the presence of God.

The same thing that brought down the glory in Solomon's day will do the same for His children today. They were praising and thanking the Lord. When you lift up your voice and your hands and your heart to the Lord, humbled in His presence, something good will happen!

When your praise goes up, His glory comes down!

A Journal of My Journey for (Date)

_____

_____

_____

_____

_____

_____

_____

_____

_____

_____

_____

_____

_____

_____

_____

_____

98. When You Pray, Believe

Mark 11:22–26 (KJV) says,
And Jesus answering saith unto them, Have faith in God. For verily I say unto you, That whosoever shall say unto this mountain, Be thou removed, and be thou cast into the sea; and shall not doubt in his heart, but shall believe that those things which he saith shall come to pass; he shall have whatsoever he saith. Therefore I say unto you, What things soever ye desire, when ye pray, believe that ye receive *them,* and ye shall have *them.* And when ye stand praying, forgive, if ye have ought against any: that your Father also which is in heaven may forgive you your trespasses. But if ye do not forgive, neither will your Father which is in heaven forgive your trespasses. (emphasis added)

Have you ever intended to pray about something and it just sort of got away from you? Maybe you even told people you would pray for them or for some needs that they brought to you. Perhaps something came up, and then something else came up. Before you know it, that prayer just never came together.

Other times maybe you do get to the prayer phase, but as soon as you get started praying, your mind starts wandering in a few dozen different directions. Prayer can become almost like a ritual, even repetitious unless you really enter into it on purpose and with a purpose.

So what is Jesus teaching us in this passage? Prayer is not just something you do with your mouth. It is something you do with your heart. You don't merely say what you are praying for, you say what you believe. Believe first and then pray. Agree with the Lord that He is ready, willing, and able to do what He said He would do and believe He will do it. When you pray, believe!

A Journal of My Journey for (Date)

99. Omnipotent God

Revelation 19:5–6 (KJV) says, "And a voice came out of the throne, saying, Praise our God, all ye his servants, and ye that fear him, both small and great. And I heard as it were the voice of a great multitude, and as the voice of many waters, and as the voice of mighty thunderings, saying, Alleluia: for the Lord God omnipotent reigneth."

When you face a situation that is beyond your ability or resources to handle, it is a blessing to have the Lord to turn to for help. That brings up a couple of questions. *Can the Lord help me? Will the Lord help me?*

To answer the second question, you can look at the question itself for guidance. The Lord *will* help if the request is according to His will!

Then you ask, "Can the Lord help me? Is He able to help me?" Of course! He is the Lord God. He's omnipotent, which means "all-ruling, absolute and universal sovereign, almighty." What a blessing to know that you serve the Almighty. There is nothing He can't do. And you? You can do all things through Christ, who gives you strength!

"Heavenly Father, I thank You for revealing Yourself to me as the almighty God, the Lord God. Help me to walk by faith and not by sight, always confessing that You are omnipotent and never doubting that You are more than able to bring me through whatever I face. I give You the glory and the honor in Jesus' name. Amen."

A Journal of My Journey for (Date)

_____

_____

_____

_____

_____

_____

_____

_____

_____

_____

_____

_____

_____

_____

_____

100. He's Alive!

Revelation 1:12–18 (KJV) says,

And I turned to see the voice that spake with me. And being turned, I saw seven golden candlesticks; And in the midst of the seven candlesticks *one* like unto the Son of man, clothed with a garment down to the foot, and girt about the paps with a golden girdle. His head and *his* hairs *were* white like wool, as white as snow; and his eyes *were* as a flame of fire; And his feet like unto fine brass, as if they burned in a furnace; and his voice as the sound of many waters. And he had in his right hand seven stars: and out of his mouth went a sharp twoedged sword: and his countenance *was* as the sun shineth in his strength. And when I saw him, I fell at his feet as dead. And he laid his right hand upon me, saying unto me, "Fear not; I am the first and the last: I *am* he that liveth, and was dead; and, behold, I am alive for evermore, Amen; and have the keys of hell and of death." (emphasis added)

What a wonderful passage from John's revelation of Jesus Christ. John was in the Spirit on the Lord's day (Sunday) when he heard the voice behind him. When he turned around, he saw the divine—except much more glorious than he had ever seen Jesus appear during the years he knew Him when He lived on the earth as a man. His eyes were like fire. His voice was like rushing water. His countenance was like the sun.

How does that compare to the Jesus before the cross? Isaiah tells us about Him. There was nothing about Jesus as a young boy and then as a young man that would have set him apart. He had no beauty or majesty to attract us to him, nothing in his appearance that we should desire. Remember, He was just the son of a carpenter!

Wow! No wonder John fell at Jesus' feet as though dead. He had never seen Jesus like this before. This is what sets Christianity apart from all false pagan religions. Our God is alive. Because He lives, He conquered death. Once Jesus rose from the dead, He took the keys to Hades (hell) and death. Jesus holds all the keys. That's why He opens doors that no human can shut. He has the key to every door!

When you look at Jesus dying on the cross, it seems like a sad thing. It seems like a defeat for all that is good. Remember, it may seem dark and hopeless right now, but Sunday is on the way! He's alive!

A Journal of My Journey for (Date)

_____

_____

_____

_____

_____

_____

_____

_____

_____

_____

_____

_____

_____

_____

_____

101. Defeating Death

First Corinthians 15:20–26 (KJV) says,
But now is Christ risen from the dead, *and* become the firstfruits of them that slept. For since by man *came* death, by man *came* also the resurrection of the dead. For as in Adam all die, even so in Christ shall all be made alive. But every man in his own order: Christ the firstfruits; afterward they that are Christ's at his coming. Then *cometh* the end, when he shall have delivered up the kingdom to God, even the Father; when he shall have put down all rule and all authority and power. For he must reign, till he hath put all enemies under his feet. The last enemy *that* shall be destroyed *is* death. (emphasis added)

The significance of the empty tomb goes all the way back to the beginning of time, back to the days of Adam, the first man. In Adam, all die. We are all born into this world under the curse of sin because of Adam's sin and because with a nature like Adam's, we have all sinned. God is love, but He is also a just God. Sin must be paid for. Either the guilty party must pay for sin, which means death, or someone has to pay the price in their place. That is what Jesus did for all who believe in Him and receive Him as Savior and Lord. All who are in Christ shall be made alive.

Jesus became the firstfruits of those who have fallen asleep—everyone who has died. One of the hardest things to deal with in this life is losing someone to death. And then there is the seeming uncertainty as to what comes after this life. All of this is answered by our Creator in His Word and demonstrated for us by our Lord Jesus Christ.

When Jesus was at the tomb of Lazarus, who had been dead for four days, He said to Lazarus's sister, Martha, "I am the resurrection and the life. He who believes in Me, though he may die, he shall live and whoever lives and believe in Me shall never die" (John 11:25 KJV).

Even though death has not yet been destroyed—that is the last enemy that will be destroyed at the end of time—Jesus has conquered death. Yes, those who trust Jesus will still die in this life, but in the life to come, we will never die. God created humankind to live forever in fellowship with Him. God's perfect creation was marred by sin, and His plan for humans was delayed until the time when the Father sent Jesus to the earth to live and die as a man.

Praise God that even though death has not yet been destroyed, it has been defeated. The empty tomb reminds us that just as our Lord lives, so we who believe and trust in Him shall live. And when this life is over, we who believe shall be kings and priests to our God. We shall wear a robe and crown all because Jesus defeated death.

A Journal of My Journey for (Date)

102. Power in the Blood

Revelation 1:5–6 (KJV) says, "And from Jesus Christ, *who is* the faithful witness, *and* the first begotten of the dead, and the prince of the kings of the earth. Unto him that loved us, and washed us from our sins in his own blood, And hath made us kings and priests unto God and his Father; to him *be* glory and dominion for ever and ever. Amen" (emphasis added).

Why did Jesus have to die such a gruesome death? Because the debt He was paying was so horrendous. His death paid the price for all the sins of the world. He willingly took our sin upon Himself on the cross. That's why the Bible says that Jesus washed us from our sins in His own blood. Jesus became sin for us so that we could become the righteousness of God in Him (2 Corinthians 5:21).

Since Jesus has washed us from our sins, we become a new creation. The cross of Christ separates the old you from the new you. It was the power of the blood of Jesus Christ that washed away your sin and made you righteous before God. Not only that, but He made you a king and priest to the heavenly Father!

Some days it may be hard to think of something to thank the Lord for. Maybe you are going through one of those seasons right now. This will always be a good way to get into a praising groove. Think about how much your heavenly Father loves you. Remember that He was willing to send Jesus into the world for the express purpose of shedding His blood in order to wash away your sins and the sins of whoever comes to Him for salvation. When He was on the cross, you were on His mind! It wasn't those spikes driven into His wrists and feet that held Him on that cross. It was love.

There is power in the blood of Jesus—power to save, power to heal, power to restore, power to deliver. It is the power of God's love poured out for you.

A Journal of My Journey for (Date)

_____

_____

_____

_____

_____

_____

_____

_____

_____

_____

_____

_____

_____

_____

_____

_____

_____

103. To Him who Sits on the Throne

Revelation 5:11–14 (KJV) says,
And I beheld, and I heard the voice of many angels round about the throne and the beasts and the elders: and the number of them was ten thousand times ten thousand, and thousands of thousands; Saying with a loud voice, Worthy is the Lamb that was slain to receive power, and riches, and wisdom, and strength, and honour, and glory, and blessing. And every creature which is in heaven, and on the earth, and under the earth, and such as are in the sea, and all that are in them, heard I saying, Blessing, and honour, and glory, and power, *be* unto him that sitteth upon the throne, and unto the Lamb for ever and ever. And the four beasts said, Amen. And the four *and* twenty elders fell down and worshipped him that liveth for ever and ever. (emphasis added)

Have you ever worried about anything? Have you been worrying about something this week or maybe even this very day? Are you worrying about something right now? Why all of the questions about worrying?

Well, for one thing, Jesus talked about worrying. That's right. We see Jesus deal with the subject of worry nine times in the Gospels. Once He asked, "Why do you worry?" and the other eight times, He said, "Do not worry."

So how does this passage from scripture help you not to worry? It is an awesome sight. The Lord has opened up a door into heaven. We see that the Lamb (the Lord Jesus Christ) is very worthy—power, riches, wisdom, strength, honor, glory, and blessing. Wow! That is a lot of worthiness! But how does that help you not to worry?

What are some of the responses associated with worry? There's pacing back and forth, fidgeting, squirming, restlessness, and a general absence of calm. In contrast, what do you see when you look through that door into heaven? You see the God of all creation sitting on His throne and with Him—the blessed Lamb of God, who takes away the sin of the world.

Now Jesus' question and His several admonitions begin to make sense. Why should you worry about anything that is beyond your control when the God who holds you and all you hold dear in His hands isn't worried about it? He is seated. He's not pacing back and forth, wringing His hands, worried about what will happen tomorrow. He knows the end from the beginning. All of your days are already known to Him, and when He thinks about you, He is only thinking about the good He wants to do for you! (Jeremiah 29:11).

So right here and right now, lay down that worry at the feet of Jesus and learn from the Lamb and from God, who sits on the throne.

A Journal of My Journey for (Date)

_____

_____

_____

_____

_____

_____

_____

_____

_____

_____

_____

_____

_____

_____

_____

_____

_____

_____

104. Throw Down that Burden

Psalm 55:22 (KJV) says, "Cast thy burden upon the LORD, and he shall sustain thee: he shall never suffer the righteous to be moved."

The word here for *burden* means "what is given." It refers to your lot in life. Since David is writing this psalm, you might think, *What would he have known about one's lot in life containing a burden or two? After all, he was the king, wasn't he?* Yes, he would one day become king, but he was not born the son of a king. Rather he grew up as a shepherd of sheep. His older brothers looked down upon him and made fun of him too.

Later he would become the archenemy of the current king (through no fault of his own), who would hunt him from cave to cave as though he were the worst enemy Israel ever had even though he was really the champion of the people who slew the giant Goliath.

Okay, so maybe he had a burden or two growing up, but let's skip ahead to the part where he is king. Surely, the time for burdens has passed by then, right? Hardly. Even a king can find that life contains burdens. One day David's own treachery would result in the death of one his most trusted men. And speaking of treachery, he would be betrayed by some of his other close friends. Eventually, people would hear him weeping loudly over the loss of his own son, who also betrayed him.

Suffice it to say that David had an understanding of the burdens of this life, but he also learned a priceless lesson. When everyone else forsakes you and you feel all alone, the Lord is always there. He will never leave you or forsake you. Therefore, when David once found himself being threatened by his own men, he strengthened himself in the Lord. In other words, you have to throw down that burden. Give it to the Lord, and He shall sustain you.

When life gets you down, cast your burden on the Lord. Throw down that burden. Jesus said to take His yoke upon you because it is easy and His burden is light.

A Journal of My Journey for (Date)

_____

_____

_____

_____

_____

_____

_____

_____

_____

_____

_____

_____

_____

_____

_____

_____

_____

105. The Battle Is Not Yours but God's

Second Chronicles 20:12–17 (KJV) says,

O our God, wilt thou not judge them? for we have no might against this great company that cometh against us; neither know we what to do: but our eyes *are* upon thee. And all Judah stood before the LORD, with their little ones, their wives, and their children. Then upon Jahaziel the son of Zechariah, the son of Benaiah, the son of Jeiel, the son of Mattaniah, a Levite of the sons of Asaph, came the Spirit of the LORD in the midst of the congregation; And he said, Hearken ye, all Judah, and ye inhabitants of Jerusalem, and thou king Jehoshaphat, Thus saith the LORD unto you, Be not afraid nor dismayed by reason of this great multitude; for the battle *is* not yours, but God's. To morrow go ye down against them: behold, they come up by the cliff of Ziz; and ye shall find them at the end of the brook, before the wilderness of Jeruel. Ye shall not *need* to fight in this *battle:* set yourselves, stand ye *still,* and see the salvation of the LORD with you, O Judah and Jerusalem: fear not, nor be dismayed; to morrow go out against them: for the LORD *will be* with you. (emphasis added)

Whenever you face a situation that is beyond your control, which is inevitable in this fallen world, it is important to remember the truth that Jehoshaphat and all of Judah learned—the battle is not yours but God's.

Let's look at how this came together. First, they acknowledge their need for help, humbling themselves before the Lord. This is always the way to approach a challenge because when you are weak, you are strong in the Lord. Judah asks God specifically for help to deal with this situation, and being honest and real with the Lord, they say, "We do not know what to do." You do not always have to have the answer for every problem. You just have to know who does and keep Him on your side!

They have acknowledged their need for God's help. They have asked for His help, and now they are waiting on the Lord. Another important point presents itself here. Tough situations that cause you to look to the Lord are excellent teaching moments for your children. All Judah stood before the Lord, not just the adults but the children and the little ones as well. These are the times that define your faith and prove who you are in Christ, and the children need to see firsthand that we never outgrow our need for God and His help.

So what comes next? We receive assurances from God and an assignment. Don't worry about a thing. Don't be dismayed at their great number. Never be intimidated by the devil's show of force. Remember that he is full of hot air! Remember that our enemy's kingdom is the kingdom of darkness and that kingdom has no power. It's just the absence of light.

Finally, we receive an assignment. Go down against them. Position yourself, stand still, and see what God does. This is how you put yourself in a position to be blessed. Humble yourself before the Lord, ask for His help, set your eyes on the Lord (not the giant), and wait for God's assurances and His assignment. Then obey the Lord, and before you know it, you will be singing, "Look what the Lord has done!"

A Journal of My Journey for (Date)

106. Possess the Land

Numbers 33:51–53 (KJV) says, "Speak unto the children of Israel, and say unto them, When ye are passed over Jordan into the land of Canaan; Then ye shall drive out all the inhabitants of the land from before you, and destroy all their pictures, and destroy all their molten images, and quite pluck down all their high places: And ye shall dispossess *the inhabitants* of the land, and dwell therein: for I have given you the land to possess it" (emphasis added).

The land of Canaan (sometimes referred to as the Promised Land) represents every promise from God. For the children of Israel, it was this land flowing with milk and honey, but for you today it could be any number of God's promises that you are waiting to see come to pass.

First, remember that God's Word is sure. If He said it, it will come to pass. He says, "When you have crossed ... into the land," not *if* but *when*. That is an important distinction, and it's one that should be a part of your vocabulary every day.

The next thing that will help you is seeing that the Promised Land is inhabited with people. You will find most often that possessing the promises of God involves confronting the enemy. He will have to be driven out of the land. This is not something that can be done by making deals with the devil and allowing him to keep a foothold in those areas of your life. Drive out the devil. Destroy and demolish everything to make room for what God has in store for you!

But will you be able to overcome the devil and destroy all of his work? The answer is very clear. "You shall dispossess the inhabitants of the land and dwell in it, for I have given you the land to possess."

Possess the land, and possess the promises of God. He has given them to you!

A Journal of My Journey for (Date)

_____

_____

_____

_____

_____

_____

_____

_____

_____

_____

_____

_____

_____

_____

_____

_____

107. Children of the King

John 1:10–13 (KJV) says, "He was in the world, and the world was made by him, and the world knew him not. He came unto his own, and his own received him not. But as many as received him, to them gave he power to become the sons of God, *even* to them that believe on his name: Which were born, not of blood, nor of the will of the flesh, nor of the will of man, but of God" (emphasis added).

There's nothing you can do about the family you are born into. You can't choose your family! Maybe you had the greatest parents on earth, or maybe they were not so great. Whatever the situation and details surrounding your earthly family, it is life-changing when you realize (and remember daily) that when you were born of God—when you accepted salvation through faith in the finished work of the Lord Jesus Christ—you became royalty. That's right—royalty. If you are a Christian, you are a child of the King.

But don't those who are a part of the royal family live in a castle and have servants and stuff? That depends on the kingdom. Jesus said, "My Kingdom is not of this world," so you are a part of the royal family but not of an earthly kingdom. You are part of the kingdom of God. So what does that do for us since we are currently living in this world?

Being a child of the King means that your heavenly Father is able to do whatever you ask. That doesn't mean the answer is always yes, but it means that if it doesn't happen right now and exactly the way you want it to, it's not because your Father isn't able. He can do anything. Being a child of the King also means that you have an awesome inheritance. It is your Father's good pleasure to give the kingdom to you. It doesn't get any better than that.

So the next time you are feeling down about your situation (maybe that's right now!), just remember that you are not who you see in the mirror or what other people think or say about you. You are a child of the King.

A Journal of My Journey for (Date)

_____

_____

_____

_____

_____

_____

_____

_____

_____

_____

_____

_____

_____

_____

_____

108. His Name Shall Be Called Mighty God

Isaiah 9:6 (KJV) says, "For unto us a child is born, unto us a son is given: and the government shall be upon his shoulder: and his name shall be called Wonderful, Counsellor, The mighty God, The everlasting Father, The Prince of Peace."

Even when Jesus' birth was being prophesied, a glimpse into His name was being revealed. You would think the occasion would call for something more ... like a newborn. But the big news wasn't that a child was born. As the angels proclaimed on that night over the fields where shepherds kept their watch, the Savior was born. But let's return to Isaiah.

Everything you need for your daily spiritual *bread* is found in Jesus. He is the bread from God who comes down from heaven (John 6:41). How does Isaiah put it here? He is called wonderful. In the Hebrew here, that means "a miracle, a marvelous thing." God is the God of wonders. He is the God of miracles. Believe Him for a miracle today!

He is the Counselor. Whenever you lack wisdom or direction, remember that you have a God who has all wisdom, knowledge, and understanding, and He says, "Ask and you shall receive"!

He is a mighty God. Have confidence in your God, who has all power and might. With God all things are possible. Do not limit God with your limited vision. Walk by faith and not by sight.

A Journal of My Journey for (Date)

_____

_____

_____

_____

_____

_____

_____

_____

_____

_____

_____

_____

_____

_____

_____

_____

109. Songs of Deliverance

Psalm 32:7 (KJV) says, "Thou *art* my hiding place; thou shalt preserve me from trouble; thou shalt compass me about with songs of deliverance. Selah" (emphasis added).

What an awesome truth King David reveals to us in this verse. All around you is a world that you cannot see with your natural eyes with things happening that you cannot hear with your natural ears. But by divine revelation, this truth is revealed to us in all its glory!

We find a place of refuge from the storms of life, a place where we can *hide* in the Lord. That doesn't mean that you get to skip all of the trials and challenges of life in this world but rather that the Lord brings you through it all and preserves you.

When three young men would not bow down and worship an idol that the king had commanded everyone to worship, they were threatened with certain death in a fiery furnace, but they were offered one more chance to give in and be like everyone else. In the natural world, you might think they should take the offer. After all, their people had been conquered and taken captive. They were nothing more than slaves in a foreign land. It would seem as if their God either could not deliver them or had chosen not to. But these young men were undaunted and told the king that their God was able to deliver them; however, even if He didn't, they would not bow down to a false god.

You may not be able to hear the song of the Lord as He surrounds you with His deliverance, but by faith you know He is always with you and helping preserve you from trouble. The fact that you are surrounded by God's deliverance means there is no way for the enemy to get you. The Lord will guard and keep that which is entrusted to Him.

So what about those three young men? They didn't bow down. Did God deliver them? He sure did, but not in the way we would think. If we could do things our way (kind of like Peter not wanting Jesus to go to the cross), we would want those young men to be delivered from the fire. But God had an even more glorious deliverance in mind. He delivered them *through* the fire! And when they came out of that trial by fire, there was not even the smell of smoke upon them. Why? Because they were sheltered safe in the arms of God.

God is singing over you right now. Oh, it might not seem like it sometimes, but you have His Word on it. He is singing a song of deliverance He wrote just for you for such a time as this.

A Journal of My Journey for (Date)

110. Stand Fast in the Faith

First Corinthians 16:13 (KJV) says, "Watch ye, stand fast in the faith, quit you like men, be strong."

Most things in this life are constantly changing. Almost everything that is living is in a constant state of flux. Children are sometimes said to be "growing like weeds," and we all know how well weeds grow! If you blink, you can miss something that's happening in the life of a child, and before you turn around, it seems, he or she is all grown up.

So you can't depend on things or people to stay the same as it relates to life. There are, however, some things that never change. God, the Creator of the world in which we live, never changes. He is the great I Am. He always is the same. When you get up each morning, you don't have to wait and see what kind of a mood He is in because He will always be as He ever was.

As a result of God's unchangeableness, His Word is also unchangeable. Heaven and earth will pass away, but His Word will never pass away. Truths from God's Word that you learned a year ago or ninety years ago are just as true today as they were then and as they were when first written. Forever God's Word is settled in heaven.

This brings us to our verse. Stand fast in the faith. In other words, let nothing move you. God never changes, and His Word never changes, so your faith never has to change or adapt to the times. You don't need a twenty-first-century faith. You need faith in God. Faith is not flexible. Faith is built on the firm foundation of the Word of God, and Jesus Christ is the chief cornerstone.

When everything around you is being tossed to and fro by the winds and waves of change, what are you to do? Stand fast in the faith!

A Journal of My Journey for (Date)

_____

_____

_____

_____

_____

_____

_____

_____

_____

_____

_____

_____

_____

_____

111. Christ in You

Colossians 1:26–28 (KJV) says, "*Even* the mystery which hath been hid from ages and from generations, but now is made manifest to his saints: To whom God would make known what *is* the riches of the glory of this mystery among the Gentiles; which is Christ in you, the hope of glory: Whom we preach, warning every man, and teaching every man in all wisdom; that we may present every man perfect in Christ Jesus" (emphasis added).

There are plenty of mysteries in the world if you think about it. The seas as well as the heavens are full of them. All around you can see God's creation reflecting His glory and at the same time reminding us how little we know and comprehend when it comes to the world around us.

But there are even more mysteries about the spiritual realm. For instance, how did God become man? How was Jesus conceived within the womb of a young woman (actually more of a girl than a woman)? How was John the Baptist filled with the Holy Spirit from birth? How does Jesus heal the sick and raise the dead? How was he raised from the dead?

There are plenty of mysteries, and the answer is always the same. "For I am the Lord, your God." When contemplating the mysteries of life, we only have to remember that God can do anything. So what about the mystery in our passage today? This is a deep one—so deep in fact that it has been hidden for ages—generation after generation. Praise God that it is no longer hidden or a mystery for those who are born again. Even Gentiles, those who were not children of God through natural means but through supernatural means, are adopted into the family of God through our Lord Jesus Christ.

So the mystery revealed is Christ in you. Because Jesus lives in you, the blessed hope of heaven is yours. You have the hope of glory.

"Heavenly Father, I thank you for adopting me into your family and making Your home in me. I thank You that my body is the temple of the Holy Spirit, that You will never leave me or forsake me. Help me to live worthy of that calling and reflect your light for everyone around me to see. In Jesus' name. Amen."

A Journal of My Journey for (Date)

_____

_____

_____

_____

_____

_____

_____

_____

_____

_____

_____

_____

_____

_____

_____

_____

112. Hold On

Isaiah 43:1–2 (KJV) says, "But now thus saith the LORD that created thee, O Jacob, and he that formed thee, O Israel, Fear not: for I have redeemed thee, I have called *thee* by thy name; thou *art* mine. When thou passest through the waters, I *will be* with thee; and through the rivers, they shall not overflow thee: when thou walkest through the fire, thou shalt not be burned; neither shall the flame kindle upon thee" (emphasis added).

One thing is for sure. Life can be a bit of a roller-coaster ride with all of its ups and downs, twists and turns. Sometimes it just seems to be chugging along at a snail's pace, and then before you know it, you seem to be in a free fall with no way to control it or slow it down.

So what is the answer? As long as you know Jesus as not only Savior but also Lord, you have His Word that He will never leave you or forsake you. You are precious in His sight, and you always have a place in the shelter of His loving arms. Well then, what about all of that fire and water? Why doesn't He just help me sail smoothly through life? There is a reason that the Father did not take us out of this world but rather allows Jesus to be with us in this world.

There are multitudes of souls that have not been redeemed. We are here to be God's witness to those who are lost. God has you here because He has a work for you to do. But what about the roller-coaster ride called life? Hold on! He who began a good work in you will see it through to completion.

When you have done everything else you are supposed to do, just hold on!

A Journal of My Journey for (Date)

_____

_____

_____

_____

_____

_____

_____

_____

_____

_____

_____

_____

_____

_____

113. A Threefold Cord

Ecclesiastes 4:9–12 (KJV) says, "Two *are* better than one; because they have a good reward for their labour. For if they fall, the one will lift up his fellow: but woe to him *that is* alone when he falleth; for *he hath* not another to help him up. Again, if two lie together, then they have heat: but how can one be warm *alone*? And if one prevail against him, two shall withstand him; and a threefold cord is not quickly broken" (emphasis added).

All the way back to the beginning of time, we see that God intended for us to have *traveling companions* on this road of life. All of His creation was *good*, and then when it came to the creation of man, it was *very good*. But then He says, "It's not good." What's not good about God's creation? It's not good that man should be alone.

Then God makes woman, and the first family is created. So we see that connections or relationships between people were created by God Himself when He gave the first man a wife. The next reference to people He would establish was to the "people of God." At first, this body included the children of Abraham, but through Jesus Christ, the family has been enlarged to include all who believe.

Through faith in Jesus, we become children of Abraham, and we become a part of the church. So once again, we are not alone in this world. We have the connection with other fellow pilgrims that God intended.

This way your reward in heaven is going to be multiplied. Think about all of the service you can do for the Lord by being a blessing to others in the household of faith. What if you have one of those times when you fall down? Your companions in the faith are there to help you up. Woe to the one who has no companions on this pilgrimage. What if you hit a dry spell and begin to cool off about the things of God? As long as you are connected to the body of Christ, the fire of others will be used by the Lord to warm you up again. And finally, there may be times when it seems you are facing the very gates of hell, but that is no match for the church.

When you need help, remember that you are not alone. Together God will make a cord that cannot be broken—in the home and in the house of God!

A Journal of My Journey for (Date)

_____

_____

_____

_____

_____

_____

_____

_____

_____

_____

_____

_____

_____

_____

114. Today's To-Do List

Here are a few things to keep on your to-do list for today (and every day)!

Proverbs 28:14 (KJV) says, "Happy *is* the man that feareth alway: but he that hardeneth his heart shall fall into mischief" (emphasis added).

Maintain an awe of God, and that will help you revere Him and keep you close to Him. How often? Always. Every day and all day long.

Let's see. What else do we have here?

First Thessalonians 5:16–18 (KJV) says, "Rejoice evermore. Pray without ceasing. In everything give thanks: for this is the will of God in Christ Jesus concerning you."

Wow! Here are three altogether. Rejoice, pray, and give thanks. How often? Always without ceasing in everything. In other words, every day and all day long.

You will be blessed if you perform the previously outlined actions, but you are also called to be a blessing, so let's review one more before we call it a day.

Hebrews 3:13 (KJV) says, "But exhort one another daily, while it is called Today; lest any of you be hardened through the deceitfulness of sin."

Here's one more thing to keep on your to-do list: You must exhort others in the Lord.

Stay humble before the Lord, acknowledge Him in all of your ways, rejoice in the Lord, pray to God, give thanks to the Lord, and exhort others in the Lord. As long as you keep these on your to-do list, you can be sure that today is going to be a good day!

A Journal of My Journey for (Date)

_____

_____

_____

_____

_____

_____

_____

_____

_____

_____

_____

_____

_____

_____

_____

_____

115. Lift Your Heart and Hands to God

Lamentations 3:41 (KJV) says, "Let us search and try our ways, and turn again to the LORD. Let us lift up our heart with *our* hands unto God in the heavens" (emphasis added).

It's never too late. As long as you have the breath of life within you, things can change! If you believe for a change in a situation or maybe in another person, the Lord may want to do something in your life.

First, search out and examine your ways. But all of the ways of a person's heart seem right to him- or herself, so how is this going to help if everything in my life looks good to me? The key here is not to examine your ways based on how they look to you but rather how they look to the Lord. How can I know what the Lord thinks of my ways? He has given us His Word. You can find everything you need to know about God's will in His Word.

To bring His Word to life, He has given us a Helper, the Holy Spirit, who will reveal even the deep things of God to us. So take a look in the mirror of His Word and listen to what the Lord is saying to you.

Okay, I see a thing or two (or three or four). Now what? There are two levels for lasting change—your heart and your hands. In your heart, the change occurs on the inside. Without a change on the inside, there can be no lasting change on the outside. Next, consider your hands.

Lift your life up to God and choose to live according to His will. If you only try to change on the outside and say, "I am never going to do this or that again," the outward change will not last.

So where does that leave us? Things can definitely change in your life starting right now. You just have to be willing to lift your heart and hands to God!

A Journal of My Journey for (Date)

116. The King of All the Earth

Psalm 47:5–8 (KJV) says, "God is gone up with a shout, the LORD with the sound of a trumpet. Sing praises to God, sing praises: sing praises unto our King, sing praises. For God *is* the King of all the earth: sing ye praises with understanding. God reigneth over the heathen: God sitteth upon the throne of his holiness" (emphasis added).

Praise is the voice of victory. When you praise the Lord, you are proclaiming who He is, what He has done, what He is doing, and what He is going to do. This passage is one of many that give us cause for praise. So as the psalm instructs, we are to praise with understanding. In fact, the more you understand the nature of God and the more you are acquainted with His ways and the more you are aware of His promises, the more you will praise Him!

Every time you learn something new about the Lord or whenever the Holy Spirit reveals something more about a scripture that you may have read a hundred times before, that gives you one more reason to praise Him.

So what can we take away from this passage of scripture? We learn that God is the King of all the earth. No matter what goes on in the world, not matter who is in charge of this or that country, God is still King of the world! No wonder that the most deranged, demon-filled dictators of our day and days past all want that position. We know that the devil desires to set up his throne in the place of God, but it will never happen. Things might seem out of control on earth from time to time (okay, maybe more often than not), but through it all God is still King of all the earth.

That's something to sing about. The God who loves you completely and has made you a joint heir with Jesus Christ is the King of all the earth. So it's time to get your praise on!

A Journal of My Journey for (Date)

_____

_____

_____

_____

_____

_____

_____

_____

_____

_____

_____

_____

_____

_____

_____

_____

117. Jesus Knows

Hebrews 4:14–16 (KJV) says, "Seeing then that we have a great high priest, that is passed into the heavens, Jesus the Son of God, let us hold fast *our* profession. For we have not an high priest which cannot be touched with the feeling of our infirmities; but was in all points tempted like as *we are, yet* without sin. Let us therefore come boldly unto the throne of grace, that we may obtain mercy, and find grace to help in time of need" (emphasis added).

Have you ever had one of those times when you feel like no one understands what you are going through or what you are feeling? Maybe you even feel as if no one really cares? Usually, if you take a step back and really look at your life, you will find there are people the Lord has put around you who truly do care and understand what you are going through—at least to some degree.

But even if you were to find yourself truly alone in your troubles and trials of life, we have God's Word that you are never alone as long as you are a follower of Christ. Notice the reason the Lord gives us here in Hebrews to hold fast. We have a High Priest, someone to speak to the Father on our behalf. Not only that, but He has passed through the heavens. Why is that important to understand? To get back to heaven, Jesus passed through this world and lived in it for more than thirty years as a man. Jesus could have stayed in heaven to begin with. After all, He was with the Father when everything was created.

So how does all of this help you in your struggles? Jesus was temped in every way that you are tempted, yet He never sinned. He qualifies to represent you in your distress because He has been there and beat it! Jesus conquered sin. He didn't just sit on His throne in heaven and declare that sin no longer existed. He came to the earth as a man and beat the devil.

Now you can always come boldly before God's throne of grace. You can ask and receive the help you need because God is merciful. He understands what you are going though. He feels your pain. Jesus knows.

A Journal of My Journey for (Date)

---

118. An Imperishable Crown

First Corinthians 9:24–27 (KJV) says,

Know ye not that they which run in a race run all, but one receiveth the prize? So run, that ye may obtain. And every man that striveth for the mastery is temperate in all things. Now they *do it* to obtain a corruptible crown; but we an incorruptible. I therefore so run, not as uncertainly; so fight I, not as one that beateth the air: But I keep under my body, and bring *it* into subjection: lest that by any means, when I have preached to others, I myself should be a castaway. (emphasis added)

At first glance, this scripture would seem to be a lesson in athletics. To be sure, there are plenty of truths that can be applied to the physical as well as the spiritual realm. You can run to win. You can control every part of your life without excess. You can be confident. You can set specific goals. You can control your body without letting it control you.

We get all of that from those few verses? Yep. And it's all good stuff—not only for runners and boxers but for everyone. These things will help you get where you want to go in life, and you'll probably get a few *crowns* along the way. You'll likely see some success in this life.

But let's not miss the point of this illustration by the apostle Paul. It's not about the crown. That's perishable. Something perishable is defined as "that which is likely to decay or go bad quickly." It has a very limited shelf life. No matter how many trophies or awards you win in this world, they will soon be gathering dust somewhere and not really have much use for you as time goes by.

It is because of this that Jesus exhorted us to lay up our treasure in heaven. When you run the race of life for an imperishable crown, you live your life for the glory of God. You seek Him and His will, and you do His will. That is truly winning the race of life. You want to hear the Lord say in that day, "Well done, good and faithful servant. Enter into the joy of your Master." That is a race well run ... and won!

So run on ... for an imperishable crown.

A Journal of My Journey for (Date)

_____

_____

_____

_____

_____

_____

_____

_____

_____

_____

_____

_____

_____

_____

_____

119. God Is Faithful

First Corinthians 10:13 (KJV) says, "There hath no temptation taken you but such as is common to man: but God *is* faithful, who will not suffer you to be tempted above that ye are able; but will with the temptation also make a way to escape, that ye may be able to bear *it*" (emphasis added).

So often it seems like the Lord gets the blame for things we go through, even though He is not at all to blame! God cannot be tempted by evil. Nor does He Himself tempt anyone (James 1:13). When Jesus came into the world, He took on the form and nature of man and became the Son of Man. He was tempted in all points as we are but without sin.

Here are a few truths to glean from our verse today.

First, everyone is tempted, and we all face the same temptations. These are common to humankind. Next, remember that God is faithful. However, even though you face temptations that at times seem to be more than you can bear, it is not God's fault. He doesn't tempt you with evil. The opposite is true. God is not the problem. He is the solution to temptation.

Finally, we see that God is always watching over us in order to deliver us when we call on Him. You can be sure that it will never be more than you are able to bear when you cast your burdens upon the Lord. If you try to deal with the devil without God's help, you will always lose! Not only that, but the Lord always has an exit strategy for you. Be sure to talk to Him about it, and don't try to figure it all out on your own.

Trust in the Lord with all of your heart. In all your ways, acknowledge Him. God is faithful!

A Journal of My Journey for (Date)

_____

_____

_____

_____

_____

_____

_____

_____

_____

_____

_____

_____

_____

_____

120. Contend for the Faith

Jude 1:3 (KJV) says, "Beloved, when I gave all diligence to write unto you of the common salvation, it was needful for me to write unto you, and exhort *you* that ye should earnestly contend for the faith which was once delivered unto the saints" (emphasis added).

Here we find Jude compelled to exhort the believers. He had wanted to write about salvation and encourage the saints in the things of God, but ungodly men crept in among the church and deceived God's people.

So what is the exhortation? As ambassadors for Christ, we are co-laborers with Him, stewards entrusted with the truth. We are to contend earnestly for the faith. But what does that mean, and how do I go about this job? Isaiah spoke of a time when "truth is fallen in the street" (Isaiah 59:14), and Paul warned of a time when people would have "itching ears" (2 Timothy 4:3) and encounter teachers that would turn them away from the truth.

Let's break down our verse a little more. Notice we are struggling for *the* faith. It is a particular, singular faith, not something new and faddish that someone came up with that sounds appealing. Even though we live in the twenty-first century, God has not and will never change. His Word has not and will never change. The truth has not and will never change.

The faith we are to contend for is the one and only faith that has been delivered to the saints. It's the truth found only in the Word of God. We contend with the devil who believes the Word and trembles at it but is set on distorting and twisting it to deceive God's children. He has been doing this since the beginning of time. There are also counterfeits and imposters who misuse the Word of God for their own purpose instead of living as servants of the Most High. They draw people to themselves and teach a biased *faith*.

But how can I be sure I am contending for *the* faith? Stick with the Word of God and always lift up Jesus. Don't follow any other *gospel* no matter how appealing it sounds or how good it makes you feel.

If God said it, believe it! Contend for *the* faith!

A Journal of My Journey for (Date)

_____

_____

_____

_____

_____

_____

_____

_____

_____

_____

_____

_____

_____

_____

_____

Well, dear fellow traveler, this brings us to the end of one portion of your journey, but there are still plenty of adventures yet to come. My prayer for you is that this devotional journal has created a hunger within you and that you will want to continue on this journey and that we can continue down that road together!

To find more devotional resources, to find links to my blogs or podcasts, to find an upcoming event or to schedule an event, please visit our website: www.thepastorspen. com.

I would love to hear how this book has had an impact on your life and any specific themes you would like to see in a future devotional journal, so please, let me hear from you!

You can help us get this and other devotional materials into as many hands and hearts as possible — spread the word to all of your family and friends. Consider giving devotional journals as gifts and give a gift that keeps on giving!

May the Lord bless and keep you, guide and direct you, and may His face shine upon you on your journey with Him. In Jesus' name, amen

Printed in the United States
By Bookmasters